A STUDY OF THE DIALECTIC OF HEGEL

A STUDY OF THE DIALECTIC OF HEGEL

B. NIRMALA DEVI

Eastern Book Linkers
DELHI : : (INDIA)

Published by :
EASTERN BOOK LINKERS
5825, New Chandrawal Road, Jawahar Nagar,
Delhi-110007

First Edition : 1995

I S B N : 81-86339-17-5

Price Rs. 350-

Printed by :
Sham Printing Agency (Amar Printing Press)
1/36A, Double Storey, Vijay Nagar, Delhi-110009

PREFACE

George Wilhelm Friedrich Hegel, the great German thinker was born at Stuttgart on August 27, 1770. Right from his school days he was an avid reader, interested in classical writers on various branches of knowledge such as mathematics, morals, etc. In 1788 he enrolled himself in Tübingen University and graduated in philosophy and classics in 1790. Later, he joined in the theological course but he left it due to his opposition to the practices of the Church. In college he devoted himself vigorously to philosophy. His fellow students in the college were Friederich Holderlin, a poet and Shelling, a philosopher.

In 1806, Hegel completed his major work *Phenomenology of Mind*, which was published in 1807. At Nūremberg Hegel published *Die objektive Logik*, the first part of his *Wissenschaft der Logik* (Science of Logic) and in 1816 he published the second part of it i.e., *Die Subjektive Logik*. This work earned him the offer of professorship at Heidelberg in 1816. In 1817 he published his *Encyclopaedia der Philosophischen Wissenschaften in Grundrisse* (Encyclopaedia of Philosophical Sciences in Outline). In 1818 Hegel accepted the offer of the chair of philosophy at Berlin, which had been vacant since Fichte's demise. After an eventful career he died on November 14, 1831.

'Dialectic' is so important and pervasive in his system that it frequents the reader at every stage in all his works.

First, the dialectic of his predecessors gets repeated by Hegel in his works for examination. He subjects it to critical scrutiny, brings out its merits and demerits. Finally after showing the inadequacies in the dialectic of his predecessors, Hegel gives his own.

One who has no background of Hegel's system, his account of dialectic with its amazing number of categories and sub-categories, is sure to get disgusted. But a sympathetic understanding of Hegel's system as a whole will not fail to disclose its significance and depth. I have taken up Hegel's dialectic for study first for the challenges it poses and second for the help it renders for better insights into philosophical problems.

(B. NIRMALA DEVI)

CONTENTS

Preface			v
Chapter I	:	Introduction	1
Chapter II	:	Dialectic in Hegel's Science of Logic	15
Chapter III	:	Dialectic in Hegel's Philosophy of Nature	69
Chapter IV	:	Dialectic in Hegel's Philosophy Spirit	94
Chapter V	:	Evalution	142
Bibliography			154
INDEX			169

CHAPTER I

INTRODUCTION

'Dialectic' is derived from the Greek term 'dialektos' which means debate or dialogue. The Greek thinkers considered 'dialectic' an art of deriving rigorous distinctions. They also considered it a science of bringing to light contradictions not known before. The application of the term 'dialectic' has been of such varied nature that no single definition can bring forth its diverse uses.

Zeno of Elea (490-430 B.C.) is considered to be the inventor of dialectic.[1] He employed 'dialectic' to show absurdities in the position of his opponent. It is through dialectic that he showed that though certain things are factually possible are logically impossible, It is on this count that Zeno showed that though motion is actually possible is logically impossible, since it involves a contradiction.[2] His famous paradoxes viz., that 'the flying arrow is at rest,' 'Achilles cannot overtake tortoise' are the outcome of his dialectical reasoning.

---

1. Zeller, Eduard, *Outlines of the History of Greek Philosophy*, Translated by L. R. Palmer, Routledge and Kegan Paul Ltd., London, VIII edition, 1931, Reprint, 1950, p. 52.
2. Hegel, *Lectures on the History of Philosophy*, Vol. I. Translated by E.S. Haldane and P.H. Simpson, Routledge and Kegan Paul Ltd., London, 1955, pp. 264-65.

For Sophists, dialectic is the rhetoric of entangling and confusing the opponent.[3] For Socrates, dialectic consists in drawing the other person to the opposite of what he believed to be correct. It is the technic of bringing home to a person that the views he held on certain conceptions are not really valid. He wanted to redeem people of their confused and wrong views on certain issues like 'justice', 'courage', 'temperance' etc.[4]

Dialectic, according to Plato, is the art of knowing through reason untouched by passion. He directs his dialectic against the general ideas of his time and to reveal the finitude of the terms of understanding.[5] It involves the comprehension of the eternal forms through reason.[6]

Aristotle considers dialectic the art of arguing consistently. He equates it with formal logic which consists in reasoning accurately from the given premises, true or false. Its concern is not so much with truth as with consistency.[7]

Hegel contends that the Greek dialectic is not wholistic, since it is confined merely to demonstrate, "the contradiction

---

3. Stace, W. T., *A Critical History of Greek Philosophy*, MacMillan India Ltd., Delhi, Ist Indian edition, 1982, p. 111.
4. Windleband, W., *History of Ancient Philosophy*, Translated by Herbert Ernest Cushman, Dover Publications, Inc. U.S.A., 1956, pp. 128-29
5. Plato, *Republic*, Translated by Francis MacDonald Cornford, Clarendon Press, Oxford, 1955, p. 534E.
6. Hegel, *Lectures on the History of Philosophy*, Vol. II, Op. cit., p. 51.
7. Taylor, A.E., *Aristotle*, Dover Publications, New York, Inc. 1955, p. 51.

and nullity of the assertions made."[8] Its defect is that it does not explain the universe as a whole. It is not of the logic of speculative thought as distinguished from understanding.* Understanding can discern only difference and fails to comprehend the unity or identity or synthesis which the speculative reason alone is capable of doing. It is incomplete and negative. It fails to go further than reducing everything, including the substantial notions to nothing, through contradiction.[9]

Hegel holds that it is Kant who has exhibited dialectic as "a necessary function of reason."[10] For Kant, the essence of dialectic consists not in reasoning as such but in an exposition of the antinomies or the necessary contradictions that arise when reason is applied to the transcendental questions viz., the origin of the world, causality, substance etc.[11] Dialectic, according to Kant, is the necessary negation of reason by itself by inventing the antinomy of its own initial position. It is the revelation of the truth that reason goes contradictory when it passes judgements about the Noumena. Kant admits that the dialectic can only expose the contradiction of reason but can never resolve it.[12]

Hegel while appreciating Kant for recognising dialectic as the intrinsic negativity of the self-moving reason, denounces

---

8. Hegel, *The Science of Logic*, Translated by A.V. Miller, George Allen and Unwin Ltd., London, 1969, p. 832.
9. Hegel, *Lectures on the History of Philosophy*, Vol. 1, Op. cit., p. 264.
10. Hegel, *The Science of Logic*, Op. cit., p. 56.
11. Kant, Immanuel, *Critique of Pure Reason*, Translated by Norman Kemp Smith, MacMillan & Co., London, 1963, pp. 217, 219, 221.
12. Ibid., p. 162.

* See page 6 for detailed discussion of the concept of understanding.

Kant for stopping reason from resolving its antinomies. He says that Kant has stopped short with the negative aspect of dialectic and made reason incapable of knowing the infinite, namely, the reasonable.[13]

Hegel brings Kantian transcendental dialectic down to the earth by extending it to the world of objects (phenomena). He characterizes the dialectic of Kant as the product of understanding and maintains that the antinomies of Kant could be resolved by the dialectic of speculative Reason.

Fichte uses dialectic in explaining the world. Fichte's dialectic involves the triadic process viz., the thesis (the Ego) which is self-consciousness, free and identical with itself; the antithesis (the Non-Ego) which is the other and the negative assertion of the thesis; and the synthesis (the unity of the two) which involves the mutual opposition of the two. Fichte calls his triad, Reality—Negation—Determination.[14]

Hegel contends that the thesis of Fichte's dialectic is purely subjective, abstract and involves undetermined identity. It lacks real objectivity, for it is fixed in its onesidedness. The transition from the thesis to the antithesis is not deduced out of necessity but merely added to it. So also the synthesis is not a determinate unity of the thesis and antithesis but a mere juxtaposition of the two.[15]

Schelling also uses dialectic in triadic form. He conceives the world or Nature as the dynamic and evolutionary process of Reason. He treats world and Reason as synonymous. Being and Spirit are one and the same. For him, the world process is dialectical in the sense that it is the unity

---

13. Hegel, *The Science of Logic*, Op. cit., p. 56.
14. Hegel, *Lectures on the History of Philosophy*, Vol. III, Op. cit., p. 409.
15. Ibid., Vol. III, p. 489

(the synthesis) of action, (the thesis) and reaction (the antithesis). He holds that there is the dialectical law of triplicity working through the world, organic and inorganic.[16]

Hegel holds that Schelling has merely presupposed the world-spirit as the synthesis of action and reaction and has failed to show it as the only truth.[17]

Dialectic, according to Hegel, does not consist in deducing the contrary to a given thesis but in seizing upon the positive in the negative. For him, dialectic is the speculation of grasping the opposites in their unity.[18] It is an organic and immanent development of the Reason from the abstract to the concrete. It is not a subjective activity, applied to the objective world externally but the necessary movement of Reason which is both the world and Spirit. Hegel regards dialectic as "the only true method"[19] which philosophy has to adopt in order to comprehend the Absolute Idea. Hegel also describes it as the spirit of contradiction that distinguishes the true from the false.[20] Let us now deal with the salient features of Hegelian dialectic.

Dialectic and Mathematics

Dialectic method is not the same as mathematical deduction. In mathematics, concepts are deduced from self-

---

16. Frederick, S. J. Copleston, *A History of Philosophy*, Vol. 7, Modern Philosophy, Part I, Fichte and Hegel, Image Books, New York, 1965, pp. 135-63, 142.
17. Hegel, *Lectures on the History of Philosophy*, Vol. III, Op. cit., pp. 525-26
18. Hegel, *The Science of Logic*, Op. cit., p. 56.
19. Ibid., p. 54.
20. Hegel, *Philosophy of Nature*, Vol. I, Translated and Edited by Petry, M.J. George Allen and Unwin Ltd., London, 1970, p. 96.

evident axioms with the help of the rules of deduction. Here, reasoning is a game of symbols without reference to actuality. Mathematical deduction is so mechanical that it can be done even by a machine. It is based on external identity. It suffers from abstract identity and tautology. It is useful to deduce definitions and precise conclusions about a dead and static world. It is conditioned by the principle of identity or difference. It is not adequate to deal with the dynamic world, since it works on the level of understanding. Hegel holds that philosophy must dispense with the method of mathematics and adopt the dialectical method of inner necessity and certainty.[21]

Dialectic and Raisonment

Hegel distinguishes his dialectic from raisonment. Raisonment is an ordinary way of argument which begins by stating facts arbitrarily selected by the author to suit his purpose. It is always based on formal identity and presuppositions. The cognition of raisonment is governed by chance and random thought.[22] Unlike raisonment, Hegel's dialectic which has notion for its soul and content, begins and ends with certainty and necessity of Reason. Hegel holds that his dialectic is the elevation of ordinary thinking and ratiocinative consciousness to the standpoint of philosophical thought.[23]

Dialectic and Understanding

Understanding (Verstand) is the mode of thinking which regards opposites as mutually exclusive. For it, each concept remains as an insulated self-existent being completely cut off

---

21 Hegel, *The Science of Logic*, Op. cit., p. 791.

22. Stace, W. T., *The Philosophy of Hegel*, Dover Publications, New York, Inc., 1955, p. 98.

23. Hegel, *The Science of Logic,* Op. cit., p. 828.

from the others. It regards them as fixed and lifeless. It approaches everything with an inflexible "either-or". Though it seeks precision and clear distinction, it cannot comprehend the whole. It fails to see identity beneath the distinctions. Hegel contends that dialectic, unlike understanding, discovers immanent and necessary connection between the fixed concepts. It is not an adventitious art of introducing semblence of contradiction into definite notion of understanding,[24] but an indwelling tendency of revealing their onesidedness and limitation. It shows the predicates of understanding in their true light. It reveals that the limitations, of the finite do not come from 'without' but dwell in the finite itself. Every finite thing contains within itself the cause of its abrogation. Man, for instance, meets death, not because of the external circumstances but because of the inherent quality, viz., mortality.[25]

Dialectic as a Process of Sublation

The dialectic is the process of the evolution of the Idea through the synthesis of opposites. For instance, the categories of being and nothing get synthesized in the category of becoming. Hegel calls the act of synthesis sublation. Sublation is a process which abolishes and preserves the differences of the thesis and the antithesis. It is the negation of the pseudo reality and the preservation of the truth of the opposites. It is neither the total annhilation nor the total retention of the opposites. It is a determinate unity in which the opposites proceed towards each other. It is a process of double determination of being ceasing-to-be and nothing coming-to-be.

---

24. Wallace, W., *Logic of Hegel*, Oxford University Press, London, 2nd edition, 1968, p. 147.

25. Ibid., p. 148.

It is not an empty determination of merely retaining or cancelling the opposites but a qualified determination of rendering the truth of the opposites explicit.[26] In the process of sublation the categories are rendered more and more concrete. For instance, prior to sublation, being and nothing are indeterminate, abstract and empty. They attain some meaning only when they are reconciled in 'becoming.' The being and nothing attain the status of 'moments' only after they are sublated as becoming.[27]

Dialectic and the Law of Contradiction

Hegel's dialectic is founded on the law of contradiction. The law of contradiction is the sine qua non of the movement of dialectic. But the law of contradiction that works through Hegel's dialectic is not the same as the traditional law of contradiction. The latter treats the opposites of contradiction as being entirely separate and mutually exclusive. It does not permit the identity of opposites. It treats contradiction as an imperfection and a contingency of subjective reflection. But Hegel regards contradiction as the determinate unity of the opposites. It involves the identity of differences and admits a proposition like 'A is A as well as not-A.' Something is and is not at the same time. Contradiction, according to Hegel, is not a negative but a positive principle of finding identity in the opposites. It is not only the nucleus of his dialectic but also "the root of all movement and vitality."[28]

Dialectic as the Movement in Triads

Dialectic is Reason evolving in triadicity, viz., thesis, antithesis and synthesis. It involves transition from abstract

26. Hegel, *The Science of Logic,* Op. cit., pp. 106-07
27. Ibid., p. 82.
28. Ibid., p. 439.

to the concrete, from indeterminate to the determinate. In the first triad, viz., being-nothing-becoming, being is the most abstract and indeterminate category. It belongs to the realm of immediate perception. Being, devoid of all qualities is equivalent to nothing. Thus being, the thesis passes to nothing, the antithesis. Nothing is not an independent category but only the 'other' of the being. Becoming is the mutual passage of being and nothing into each other. In comparison with being, nothing is more concrete, for it involves the comprehension of being, in its otherness, viz., negativity. In comparison with nothing, becoming is still more concrete, for it includes both being and nothing within itself. The dialectic does not stop here but proceeds further and further through more and more specific triads till it reaches the most concrete category viz., the Absolute Idea which preserves all the previous categories.

Dialectic and the Law of Identity and the Law of Excluded Middle

Hegel's dialectic abandons the law of identity and the law of excluded middle. He says that the law of identity is devoid of content, for it merely asserts that "something is something" (A is A). Its predicate does not reveal anything new but repeats what is there in the subject. Hegel condemns it as "the expression of an empty tautology."[29] Nevertheless, Hegel maintains that the law of identity contains within itself the law of contradiction. The proposition "a tree is a tree" implies not only the knowledge of the tree as tree but also the knowledge of all that is different from the identity of the tree to itself. The tree is understood in opposition to everything that is not tree. The law of contradiction is the explication of the hidden contradiction of the law of identity.

---

29. Hegel, *The Science of Logic*, Op. cit., p. 81.

Hegel treats the law of excluded middle which states that everything is either positive or negative as "triviality leading nowhere"[30] for it denies the posibility of the third alternative. It admits the oppossition or identity between the alternatives separately but not the contradiction of accommodating the difference and identity between them at a time. Hegel at the same time contends that the law of excluded middle, when grasped in its necessity, reveals that it carries within itself the spirit of contradiction of relating the subject not only to one of the alternatives but also to both. The proposition 'A is either P or Q' could also be 'A is both P and Q.'

Determinateness as the Distinction of the Dialectic

Dialectic begins with being and ends with the Absolute Idea. But the being which is at the beginning of the dialectic is indeterminate. Neverthless being is not a mere abstraction but the 'totality' endowed with the urge to carry itself further. Although the being, as such, does not contain in itself the Absolute Idea, it has the potentiality to evolve into the Absolute Idea through this dialectical movement of Reason. The absolute is the consummation of the being. So the advancement of the being towards Absolute Idea is not an accident but a necessity. The method is not a formal affair; it is not something posited in external reflection but a determinate development of thought from being to the Absolute Idea.[31]

Dialectic as the Absolute Method

Hegel regards dialectic as an absolute method, since it is founded on the absolute cognition of thought "a super-sensuous inner intuition",[32] which cognizes itself by means of

30. Hegel, *The Science of Logic*, Op. cit., p. 438.
31. Ibid., p. 829.
32. Ibid., p. 828.

itself in everything. It considers things in and for themselves and brings before consciousness what is immanent in them. It dispenses with the finite cognition which emphasizes diversity and presupposes the objective world as something given. Dialectic is such an absolute force that nothing can either penetrate or resist it. Anything is comprehended in its truth only when it is completely subjugated to dialectic. Hegel says, "The absolute method, on the contrary, does not behave like external reflection but takes the determinate element from its own subject matter, since it is itself the subject matter's immanent principle and soul."[33]

Dialectic as the Unity of Form and Content

Generally, a method is considered the form of a given content. The content is assumed as given to the method. The method is treated as having an external and contingent relation to its content. But Hegel's dialectic stands for the unity of content and form, since it is synonymous with its subject matter, viz., the self-knowing notion. Dialectic is the concrete existence which is notion itself. It is the movement of notion which is a pure correspondence of itself and its reality. It is the self-determining and self-realizing absolute activity of notion itself. Thus dialectic bridges the gap between logic and metaphysics. Hegel's system of thought is both logic and metaphysics. For it knowing and being are one and the same. So also things and thoughts or existence and reason are one and the same. The subject and object are synonymous.[34]

Omnipresence of Dialectic

As already mentioned, dialectic is the universal and irresistable power of Reason working in everything. It is the

---

33. Hegel, *The Science of Logic*, Op. cit., p. 830.
34. Marcuse, Herbert, *Reason and Revolution*, Routledge and Kegan Paul Ltd., London, 1954, pp. 65-66.

movement of Reason which transforms the implicit into explicit and immediacy into mediacy. Apart from its general applicability, the presence of the dialectic can be felt in all natural processes, like, the movement of heavenly bodies, physical elements and meteorological changes. Hegel holds that the changes in Nature are dialectical. He maintains that dialectic is present in the human affairs like law and morality. He is of the view that the fact 'extreme despotism and extreme anarchy change into each other' and the sayings like 'pride comes before a fall' and 'too much wit outwits itself' smacks of dialectics. The facts that extremes of pain and pleasure pass into each other, the deepest sorrow is betrayed by a smile and the deepest happiness finds relief in tears stand a testimony to the dialectical nature of even bodily and mental feelings.[35]

The Dialectical and the Historical

The dialectical movement of thought is not mystical. It is neither arbitrary nor accidental but a necessary movement in time. Its categories correspond to the essential standpoints of the various systems of philosophy. That is, each conception of a particular system finds a corresponding place as a category in the dialectic of Logic. For instance, the dialectic of Logic begins with the category of being which was the governing conception of the ancient Greek Philosophy of Parmanides. The category of becoming was an essential concept of the Philosophy of Heraclitus. The category of being-for-self was the central concept of the Atomists. And the category of the substance corresponds to the concept of substance in the Philosophy of Spinoza. Thus dialectical evolution of the Idea stands for the evolution of Philosophies

---

35. Wallace, W., *Logic of Hegel*, Op. cit., p. 151.

in history. The systems of Philosophy are not a chance product but the result of the rational evolution of the Idea in the successive systems. The Idea as 'being' begins with the Philosophy of Parmanides, passes through various other systems and attains the status of the Absolute in the system of Hegel himself. The absolute includes and transcends all the categories that precede it. So also Hegel's Philosophy includes and transcends all the previous systems of Philosophy. In short it is the consummation of the whole history of Philosophy. The history of the world is governed by the Idea. It is the dialectical self-manifestation of the Idea in time.[36]

The present work proposes to study Hegel's dialectic in its three spheres, viz., Logic, Nature and Spirit.

Introduction gives a brief account of the concept of dialectic, in Western Philosophy. It brings out dialectic as understood by the thinkers like, Zeno, Sophists, Socrates, Plato etc., and Hegel's objections raised against them. It forms the first chapter.

Dialectic in Hegel's Science of Logic, the second chapter, presents Hegel's dialectic as it is expounded in his *Science of Logic*. It deals with Reason in its 'abstraction.' It expounds Reason in pure thought or as it works in the individual's mind. Depending upon the main triad of Logic, the chapter is divided into three divisions, namely, Being, Essence and Notion.

Dialectic in Hegel's Philosophy of Nature, the third chapter, deals with dialectic as it manifests itself in Nature and as presented in Hegel's *Philosophy of Nature*. It describes Reason as it unconsciously works through Nature. The chapter is divided into three sections namely, Mechanics, Physics and

36. Stace, W. T., Loc. cit., pp. 31-32.

Organics which constitute the main triad of the Philosophy of Nature.

Dialectic in Hegel's Philosophy of mind or Spirit, the fourth chapter, gives a detailed account of dialectic as it is embodied in the *Philosophy of Spirit*. It depicts Reason as it is consciously expressed through human institutions like state, religion, arts and philosophy. It studies reason as it evolves from the 'soul'—the most abstract state of Absolute Spirit to the Absolute Spirit which is concrete. The discussion centres round the three divisions, viz., (1) Subjective Spirit (2) Objective Spirit and (3) Absolute Spirit.

Evaluation is devoted to the appraisal of Hegel's dialectic. It forms the fifth chapter of the present work.

CHAPTER II

DIALECTIC IN HEGEL'S SCIENCE OF LOGIC

Introduction

As has been discussed in the previous chapter, the aim of Hegel is to deduce the world logically from the first principle, namely, Idea or Reason. He does not dogmatically assert the existence of the world as a mere fact but demonstrates why the world must be such as it is. Hegel deduces the world not as an effect from cause but as a consequent from an antecedent. The deduction passes through three stages, viz., Logic, Nature and Spirit. Logic gives an account of the first principle, viz., Idea or Reason as it is in-itself. Nature deals with Reason in its otherness. And Spirit deals with Reason in and for-itself.

The present chapter is devoted to the exposition of Hegel's Idea as it manifests in the sphere of Logic. In Logic Reason evolves from the most abstract, undifferentiated and distinctionless concept to the most concrete, distinct and self-differentiating one. In it Reason passes through the main triad, viz., Being, Essence and Notion. Being constitutes the Idea as understood by common sense. Here Idea is treated in terms of mere qualities and quantities. Essence constitutes the Idea as regarded by science and understanding. Here the Idea is understood in terms of cause and effect, substance and attributes. Notion, comprehension of Idea by philosophy wherein the Idea is revealed as a living spiritual organism, is consummated in the form of the world.

Section A

BEING

Now let us deal with the sphere of being. As already mentioned, the Idea in the realm of being is comprehended in its immediacy and crudeness. It stands for the most elementary knowledge about the Idea. Accordingly, the being gets divided into the triad, viz., quality, quantity and measure.

(i) *Quality* : But quality* is not the first category of the sphere of Being. Hegel divides quality into the traid, viz., being, determinate being and being-for-self. He treats being, the sub-category of quality as the first category of the realm of Being.** According to Hegel Reality in its most immediate and abstract stage can be defined only as being. Here being stands for the mere 'isness' of everything. It is devoid of all determinations. It is the utter emptiness of all that exists.

---

* Hegel uses the term "quality" in two senses. First, he uses it as the name of the general sphere representing all the categories in the realm of being. Second, he uses it as the name of the specific category which is a subcategory of the category called determinate being.

** Hegel uses the term "Being" in three different senses. First he uses it as the thesis of the main triad, viz., Being, Essence and Notion. Second, he uses it as the thesis of the triad, viz., being, determinate being and being-for-self. Third, he uses it as the thesis of the triad, viz., being, nothing and becoming. Hegel begins his Logic with the category of being, since the Reality was first defined as being by Parmanides. Philosophy, according to Hegel, is a history of systems which have defined Reality at various stages of its development. He believes that Reality unfolded itself in successive systems and attained its fulfilment in his own system. He holds that the essential concept of each system finds its proper place in the system of his philosophy.

It speaks of the absolute minimum of knowledge about that which exists. For Hegel, to know an object merely as 'being' is to know next to nothing about it. Being "is pure indeterminateness and emptiness. There is nothing to be intuited in it, if one can speak of intuiting or it is only this pure intuiting itself,......"[1]

Being passes into its opposite, namely, nothing. Being is the 'isness' which cannot be perceived by senses. It is mere abstraction which is empty thinking. It is pure indetermination and vacuity that cannot be taken to be something. It is devoid of all content. So being can be called nothing as well. Being is equivalent to nothing. This nothing, according to Hegel, is not a non-entity but an emptiness devoid of all determinations like size, shape, weight, colour, etc. Hegel says "Nothing is simply equality with itself, complete emptiness, absence of all determinations and content, undefferentiatedness in itself."[2]

Thus the being of an object is comprehended as nothing. So the thought of being is the same as the thought of nothing. But to define Reality as being and nothing is merely to affirm its 'isness'. It does not provide any answer to the question. 'What is Reality ?'

Being and nothing are absolutely identical. They are so equal as the sides of an equation. Just as every equation can be reversed, so also being and nothing are interchangeable. If, A=B, then B=A. Similarly, if being=nothing, then nothing =being. Thus being and nothing pass into each other. Hegel calls, this passage of being and nothing into each other 'becoming'. Becoming is the concrete unity of being and

---

1. Hegel, *The Science of Logic*, Op. cit., p. 82.
2. Ibid., p. 82.

nothing. It is a unity since it involves the identity of being and nothing. The unity is concrete in the sense that it contains the difference of being and nothing within it. The very idea of passage implies that being and nothing are still different. Passage of one into another would not be possible without difference. The idea of becoming implies that something becomes something different from itself. A cannot become A. It must become only B. Thus becoming includes the identity as well as the difference of being and nothing.

Depending upon the mutual passage of being and nothing, the category of becoming passes into its two sub-categories, namely, origination and decease. Origination is the passage of nothing into being and decease is the passage of being into nothing. Hegel describes origination as coming-to-be and decease as ceasing-to-be. The idea as becoming is a mere indeterminateness. It is in a state of flux. But it soon finds itself in a state of rest. It collapses like the flame which gets extinguished when it consumes its content. The state of rest is the being which does not any more pass into its opposite, nemly, nothing. Hence, the being now is definite. It is so and not otherwise. Hegel calls this category determinate being. The determinate being represents only a general idea of determination. That is, at this stage, it is possible only to know that a thing has some colour but not a specific one. The determinateness is that which prevents a thing from disappearing into nothing. It is identical with the actuality of being. The destruction of it would mean the destruction of the being of a thing. Hegel names this inseparableness of determinateness and being as quality, Hegel says, "Determinateness thus isolated by itself in the form of Being is quality which is wholly single and immediate."[3]

3. Hegel, *The Science of Logic*, Op. cit., p. 111.

Quality passes to being-in-itself and being-for-other. The quality can be regarded in its positive aspect. It constitutes the reality of a thing. It exists in itself apart from all other things. For example, a thing with a certain specific gravity, supporting cumbustion and without odour constitutes the thing called oxygen. Hegel calls it being-in-itself. At the same time quality possesses a negative aspect also. It determines a thing as not being some other thing. It represents the character of a thing as negating some other thing. For example, the qualities which make a thing 'table' also make it not a 'wall'. Hegel calls it being-for-other.

Quality of necessity, makes a thing limited. A thing having a certain quality is limited by it. To be qualified, to be determined and to be limited are one and the same. Here, Hegel observes the principle, viz., all determination is negation. For example, to determine a meadow as meadow is to negate it as not being a pond and to limit it only to meadow. Hegel calls it the limit.

To be limited means that a thing is related to itself as something negative. It 'is' in not being something else. Therefore the limit strives to destroy itself and becomes something different. It perishes the moment it is born and becomes an other limited thing. This Hegel calls the finite. To be limited means to be finite. To be finite implies that there is something beyond the finite. This gives rise to two conceptions, viz., "something" and "other". The "other" is that which is beyond "something". It can also be "something" and the "something" can also be the "other". They are identical and each passes into the other. This passage is alteration. Alteration is change of quality as when a leaf changes its colour or a man grows old. In alternation, one finite perishes and becomes an other finite which again becomes yet an other finite and the process goes on ad infinitum. Consequently, there is an infinite series of finites.

Hegel says, "The progress in infinity is consequently, only the perpetual repetition of one and the same content, one and the same tedious alteration of this finite...."[4] This Hegel calls the spurious infinite, e.g., infinite numerical series. Spurious infinite is an endless reciprocal determination of one finite by the other. In it, one finite perishes into another and in the process changes itself into its opposite. It is by perishing itself, that the finite consummates its true potentialities. This constant perishing is the constant negation or determination of the finite by itself. Hegel calls this process of self-determination or negation of the finite through perishing the true infinite. "The infinite then is precisely the inner dynamic of the finite, comprehended in its real meaning. It is nothing else but the fact that finitude exists only as a passing beyond itself."[5]

Now, the determinate being, the antithesis of the category of being passes to the synthesis, namely, the being-for-self. We have seen so far how the determinate being gives rise to the finite which perishes itself perpetually. The finite is seen as the 'infinite' process of transformation. It is this infinite process of transformation that Hegel calls being-for-self. He takes self-consciousness as the nearest example of being-for-self. Being-for-self is a process but never a state. It integrates all its external conditions with its proper being. It passes beyond its otherness in such a manner that it is infinite return upon itself Natural things can never be being-for-self. They always remain to be being-for-other. Being-for-self is free whereas the being-for-other is not free.[6]

---

4. Hegel, *The Science of Logic*, Op. cit., p. 142.
5. Marcus Herbert, *Reason and Revolution*, Op. cit., p. 138.
6. Ibid., p. 140.

Being-for-self yields its triad viz., the one, the many and repulsion and attraction. Being-for-self is a being which is self-subsistant. It is purely for-itself. It is not related to anything other than itself. It is that which has absorbed its other into itself. In it, the distinction between itself and its other is annulled. Thus the being-for-self is a single unity. Hegel calls this a one. The unity of the one is not empty but absolute, since it implies an independence of anything other than itself.

The one passes to the many or many ones. The one is self-related. It means that the one is related to itself. It involves the distinction between the one which is related and the one to which one is related. Thus the one creates another one within itself. Then there are two ones which have their own ones. Thus, the one suffers self-diremption into a multiplicity of ones which Hegel calls the many. The many passes to repulsion and attraction. The process by which each one excludes the other is called repulsion, and the process by which each one includes the other is called attraction. The repulsion and attraction reveal respectively the identity and difference of the many ones. Now the categories of attraction and repulsion pass to the category of quantity.

(ii) *Quantity* : Repulsion is the difference between the two ones and attraction is their identity. But the relation between any two ones is both of difference and identity at the same time. That is, the two ones repulse and attract each other simultaneously. Thus attraction and repulsion become identical. "The relation of one to the other one (repulsion) is only its relation to itself (attraction). The distinction between attraction and repulsion thus collapses to unity. The two coalesce into one. This unity of attraction and repulsion is quantity."[7] The quantity gets divided into pure quantity, quantum and degree. Pure quantity is indefinite but not infinite like time in general or men in general. Pure quantity of time or men implies that there is an indefinite length of time or an indefinite number of men but not infinite length of time or infinite number of men. Quantum is a definite quantity such as five minutes, twenty men, a hundred degrees of temperature etc. The pure quantity becomes quanta when we carve out of the former a definite number as when one carves out fifty or thousand men out of the indefinite number of men. Pure quantity is nothing but a series of ones. It is one, one, one...etc. The ones in pure quantity are identical. They attract each other. The principle of attraction joins them together and forms a continuity. Hegel calls this continuous quantity continuous magnitude. At the same time, the one are different from each other. The principle of repulsion disjoins them. Now the quantity is discontinuous or disconnected ones. This is discrete magnitude. Thus every quantity is both continuous and discrete magnitude. So space, which is pure quantity is both continuous and discrete. It is continuous, since every part of it runs into its other. It is discrete, for it is composed of miles, feet, inches, etc., which divides it. That is, the many ones in pure quantity are both continuous and discrete. So, we may take a certain number of ones and put them together. We may also cut off a certain number of ones and separate them from the rest and put a limitation on quantity. Hegel calls it limitation of quantity.

As already mentioned, quantum is putting a limitation on pure quantity. Quantum is making quantity definte and determinate. Quantum is an aggregate. It is a many or a plurality. Basing on discretion, quantum is a sum of many

---

7. Stace, W. T. Loc. cit., p. 154.

ones and basing on continuity, it is a unity of many ones. The factors of sum and uuity make a number. For instance, it is by taking sum unity of seven ones that we make a single quantum.

Hegel holds that the category of number is the perfect expression of quantum, for it is only by number that we limit pure quantity. It is only by counting an indefinite number of men that we arrive at a quantum. Reducing pure quantity to quantum is giving it a definite number.

Then the category of quantum with its extensive magnitude passes to the category of intensive magnitude which is degree. Extensive magnitude of quantum implies a series of units which are external to each other. The units in extensive magnitude lie outside one another. For example, in a ten feet of space, each foot is external to all the other feet. In a group of hundred men, each man is separate from others. But the degree is that in which the units do not lie outside each other but merge with the limiting one. The units become internal to the limiting one. They get absorbed within the unity of the limit. Hegel takes a hundred degrees of temperature, a hundred degrees of brilliancy in light, a certain degree of intensity in colour as examples of the degree. In a hundred degrees of temperature, the constituent degree, say, the 99th degree or the 98th, cannot exist by itself. The constituent degrees lie outside the hundredth degree which is the limit. There only the hundredth degree exists and the others get absorbed within it. To put it simply, "Extensive magnitude is a manifoldness. It is in itself multiple. Intensive magnitude is not thus multiple within itself. It is a simple undifferentiated unity, a simple determinateness."[8]

---

8. Stace, W.T., Loc. cit.,p. 162.

The degree passes to its subsequent categories namely, the quantitative infinite progress and the quantitative ratio. We have seen how an indefinite quantity of necessity becomes a quantum and a degree. The twentieth degree, for example, is a definite quantity and therefore a quantum. Degree depends upon the factor of continuity by virtue of which the other ones are identical with the l imiting one. And by virtue of the same factor of continuity the ones within the limit, viz., one, two, three, etc., upto twenty, are identical with the ones beyond the limit, i.e., twenty-one, twenty-two, etc. Thus the limit is broken down. Then the quantum passes beyond its limit into the indefinite quantity which again becomes a quantum. This new quantum again transcends its limit and passes into indefinite quantity beyond, which again becomes a third quantum and so on ad infinitum. Hegel calls this infinite series of quantum the quantitative infinite progress.

We have seen so far that there is an infinite series of quantum. One quantum passes into the other continuously. That is, one quantum determines the other. Hegel calls it a spurious infinite of the category of quantity. This passes to real infinite when each quantum determines itself. The deduction is as follows. One quautum passes into another. That is, one determines the other. The principle of continuity renders one quantum the same as the other. So in determining one by the other, each quantum determines itself. It is precisely the idea of self-determination that changes the category of quantitative infinitive progress into quantitative ratio. The conception of ratio has two sides, viz., (1) two quanta whidh are related to each other; (2) single quantum which is formed by the coalescence of the two quanta. The two aspects are identical with each other. For example, we have an equation like, 6 : 3=2 in which on one side there are two quanta related to each other and there is a single quantum on the other. In fact, the second aspect, namely, the single quantum namely 2 is the first aspect, namely, the two quanta namely 6 : 3 coalesced to one.

In ratio, the quantum is seen as determining itself internally and all such internal determination, according to Hegel, is quality. For instance, in the equation 6 : 3=2, the 6 : 3 is quantitative, since it is an external relation of two quanta. The '2' is qualitative, since it is a self-determined and self-related quantum. It is a being-for-self that can change the other side of the equation but not vice versa. That is, the internal relation can determine the external relation but not vice versa. For example, in the equation 6 : 3=2, the 6 : 3 can be changed indefinitely as 12 : 6 or 120 : 60 etc., without changing 2. The '2' can still remain as it is. But the '2' cannot be changed without the corresponding change on the other side. The '2' can be made '3' only when we alter the 12 : 6 as 9 : 3. Thus the self-determination of a quantum is qualitative in character, for it brings about change in the very being. Thus we now notice quantity when developed as ratio passes back into quality. But it is a quantity which is qualitative as well. It is the synthesis of quantity and quality. Hegel calls it measure.

(iii) *Measure* : Measure can be defined as "the dependence of quality upon quantity."[9] For example, water when heated beyond a certain temperature, changes its quality and becomes steam. It becomes ice when cooled beyond a certain measure. Measure, like other categories, is a definition of the absolute wherein quality and quantity affect each other. Hitherto, quantity was seen as being utterly indifferent to and independent of quality. It was defined as an external determination to the being of the thing. It could be altered

9. Stace, W.T., Loc. cit.. p. 169.

without altering the quality of the thing. But, the dialectic in measure shows that quality and quantity are no more different but each involves the other. The category of measure falls into its sub-categories, namely, (1) the specific quantum, (2) the measureless, (3) the infinite of measure. The specific quantum is a certain definite quantum which constitutes a limit within which quality remains unaltered though quantity varies. The specific quantum speaks of the loose connection between the quality and quantity. In it, there is no absolute dependence of quality and quantity on one another. Here, the dependence is only relative and the unity is immediate. Complete unity would mean that any change whatever in quantity would be followed by a change in quality. This is absent in the specific quantum. For example, the quantum of temperature may vary as it pleases upto the limit of 100° without the quality undergoing any change. But beyond the limit of 100° the quality of liquidity suddenly disappears and the water becomes gaseous.

The category of specific quantum passes to the category of measureless wherein the quantity is treated as being completely independent of quality. In specific quantum we have a quantitative limit. The quantitative limit does not remain so far ever. Our experience shows that the quantity must for ever transcend itself irrespective of qualitative changes. Thus we have quantity which is completely unattached to quality. This Hegel calls the measureless. In measure there is the attachment of a quality to a quantity whereas in measureless such attachment is totally absent.

Now the measureless passes to the infinite of measure. In measureless, the quantity has appeared to be free of quality. But the quantity cannot for ever remain independent of quality. The quantity of necessity returns to quality. It cannot subsist by itself. It becomes again attached to quality. The attachment of quantity to quality is measure. Thus the measureless passes into measure which in turn passes into measureless. This new measureless again returns to measure and the process goes on ad infinitum. Thus we have an infinite series of measure and measureless. This Hegel calls the spurious infinite of measure. But the measure and the measureless in determining each other, they, in fact, determine themselves. For measure and measureless are synonymous. "The measure in passing into the measureless only passes into itseif, for the measureless turns out to be itself a measure."[10] Hegel regards this infinity as the true infinite of measure which involves the absolute unity of quality and quantity.

In the sphere of Being, everything is considered in its independence and immediacy. The mind which is under the spell of Being is confined to common sense and immediate perception. Here, the Absolute is known as being 'there'; things are considered mainly in terms of quality and quantity. For example, a thing is immediately known only to be either as real or big. To start with, the quality and quantity appeared to be different. But the dialectic shows that the categories of quality and quantity are not separate but indissolubly linked together. In fact, thought passes from one category to the other, since the categories are interdependent. But, in the realm of Being, the interdependence of the categories was implicit and had to be explicated. This explication takes place in the next category i.e , Essence.

---

10. Stace, W.T., Loc. cit., p. 175.

Section B

ESSENCE

As has been mentioned, the realm of Being is characterised by immediacy. Its categories are simple and self-subsistent. They are immediate in the sense that they do not explicitly refer to any other category. They do not mediate each other on their own. The dialectical march of Reason reveals that they are not self-sufficient but dependent on one another. It breaks down the apparent disconnections and establishes inner connections between them. Indeed, dialectical method is the critical examination which renders implicit mediation between the categories explicit.

Thus the sphere of Essence stands for mediation and explicitness. Its categories explicitly mediate one another. They always appear in pairs. They are correlative like cause and effect, substance and accident, identity and diversity, positive and negative, action and reaction etc. Here, each term explicitly refers to the other. The one cannot be conceived independently of the other. As Stace has rightly put it, "The categories of being are like single stars which appear to be self-governed but in reality form parts of one vast system of universal attractions. Their connection with the others is implicit, hidden. The categories of essence resemble those double stars which are linked together and revolve round each other. In their case the connection is open and explicit."[11]

The categories of Essence supersede those of Being in that they give a more adequate knowledge of the idea. In Being the comprehension of the Idea is confined to an unreflective common sense and immediacy. In Essence the Idea

11. Stace, W.T., Loc. cit., pp. 124-25.

is understood in terms of the categories used in science like cause and effect, substance and accidents, positive and negative, action and reaction etc. Hegel holds that the categories of Being stand for the simple apprehension of the Idea. They correspond to the terms in formal logic. That is, they stand for the definitions of the Idea in simple terms which represent the self-identical and self-subsistant entities. They hardly reveal anything about the Idea. To say that the Idea is being or nothing or quality or quantity is to say next to nothing about it. But the categories of Essence correspond to the judgements of formal logic which define a thing by connecting it with its essential nature.

A judgement is constituted by a simple term split into two terms which are related by copula. For example, the term 'man' necessarily refers to its related term 'mortality' and gives rise to the judegment 'man is mortal'. So also Idea in Essence is comprehended in relation to its essential nature. Thus all judgements involve reflection. So also the standpoint of Essence as against that of Being, is the standpoint of reflection.[12] To say that the Idea is substance and accident or cause and effect is to say 'something' about it,

The categories of Being are simple, abstract and incomplete and their connections are only external, whereas the categories of Essence are more precise, methodical, distinct and can no longer be interpreted in terms of objective qualities and quantities. The latter are intrinsically connected with its opposite inherent within itself. Thus when compared to Being, Essence is one step closer to the realization of the Absolute.[13]

In Essence, dialectic as a critical contemplation reveals self-contradiction as the universal ontological law, It shows

12. Hegel, *The Science of Logic*, Op. cit., p. 391.
10. Marcuse, Herbert, Loc. cit., p. 70.

that everything in the world is self contradictory in itsself-identity and vice versa. The reality is revealed to be a movement of transition between identity and difference or negation. Thus, in Essence, the grip of common sense confined to identity is overcome and the reality is comprehended in relation to its opposites.[14]

The Idea proceeds to the transition of Being with its ultimate sub-category of infinite of measure and to Essence. As already mentioned, the infinite of measure is the absolute unity of quality and quantity. In it, the quality and quantity are identical and interchangeable. But the fact that they are interchangeable necessarily implies that they are different also. Thus the category of infinite of measure reveals Being as having to strata, namely, identity and difference. The outer stratum stands for the diversified Being constituted by the difference of quality and quantity. The inner stratum stands for the unchanging unity of Being constituted by the identity of quality and quantity. Now the Being is revealed as having not only the outer rind like quality, quantity, and measure but also the inner rind namely the Essence. The two strata are related to each other. One necessarily refers to the other. Thus in Essence the being is known not just as qualities, quantities and measure which belong to the outer layer of the being but comprehended as an essential being which supports the immediate being which is not essential but contingent. Thus Essence stands for the universal relativity wherein a being is revealed to have a 'double' being.[15] The realm of Essence comprises three spheres, namely, (1) essence as ground of existence, (2) appearance and (3) actuality.

---

14. Marcuse, Herbert, Loc. cit. pp. 146-47
15. Stace, W. T., Loc. cit., p. 176

(i) *Essence as Ground of Existence* : The essence as ground of existence has its own sub-categories, viz., (1) the categories of reflection, (2) existence, and (3) the thing. Let us now deal with the categories of reflection. Hegel regards identity, difference and the group as the categories of reflection the deduction of which is as follows.

Hegel begins the study of reflection with the category of identity. As already mentioned, a thing is known in terms of appearance and reality which is essence. But the appearance is not different from the reality. One depends on the other. They together constitute one thing. The perfect equality between two sides of the relation gives the category of identity. For example, 'p' depends on 'q' and 'q' depends on 'p'. The two sides of relations are identical with each other. The two sides are not two things, but they are two sides of one thing. Hence essence is appearance. So, the relation of the essence to the appearance is only the relation of the essence to itself. Hence essence is self-relation. This reflex or self-relation is self-identity. Hegel says, "This identity becomes an identity in form only, or of the understanding, if it be held hard and fast, quite aloof from difference."[16] The concept of identity passes to the concept of difference, since the former necessarily implies the latter. Identity means a relation between two entities, the subject and predicate which are different from each other. When we say that 'X' is 'X', it also means that the subject 'X' is different from the predicate 'X'. So the category of identity which is a relation of essence to self necessarily implies that it is a negative self-relation. It involves the difference between the entities related. The category of difference has within it three sub-categories, viz., variety, likeness and unlikeness, and positive and negative.

16. Wallace, William, Loc. cit., pp. 212-13

Variety implies the relation of object to a plurality of objects. It is an external relation in which things are indifferent to each other's being. The change in the one is indifferent to the other. For example, a table is related to diversified things like horse, stone, etc. The table is different from a horse or a stone. In this, there is no specific relation of opposition except that of difference. The change in the table does not bring about a change in the stone. This is called variety or diversity which proceeds to a more concrete category, viz., likeness and unlikeness.

In variety, a thing has a relation to any other thing. That is, a pencil is related to a hill, a car, a man, a camel, and so on. In it there is no need for comparison. It is a category of mere difference. But in likeness and unlikeness we compare things that are alike, like horse and zebra. Likeness is identity and unlikeness is difference between two things. The horse and zebra are alike and unlike at the same time. This passes to the category of positive and negative.

Just as identity and difference involve each other, so also likeness and unlikeness involve each other. They are interdependent. At the same time they are different from each other. Here we have a kind of difference in which the likeness and unlikeness are mutually dependent and firmly bound to each other. This relation of difference is called positive and negative or contrariety by Hegel. The degree of difference in positive and negative is more specific than that of likeness and unlikeness. As Wallace puts it, "The positive is the identical self-relation, in such a way as to be the negative, and the negative is the different by itself so as not to be the positive."[17] Now difference along with its sub-categories passess to the category of ground.

---

17. Wallace, William, Loc. cit., p. 219

As said above, the categories of positive and negative depend mutually on each other. The positive is positive only in reference to the negative and negative is negative only in reference to the positive. Since they have identical relation with each other, one may be substituted for the other. Here we must take the consciousness of this relation into consideration. The consciousness of darkness is as much positive as that of light and the consciousness of light is as much negative as that darkness. Hence each is identical with and absolutely dependent on the other. The negative depends completely on positive and vice versa. Each is equally the ground of the other. Hegel calls this the category of ground. The identity in the ground is a relation of self-to-self. Hegel says that a ground can exist only as the ground of something. But that which is grounded is the ground itself......The grounded and the ground are of the same content. The difference between them is a simple relation of self to self which is mediation.[18] The ground dialectically moves to the category of existence.

In ground, the one which is ground is identical with the one which is the grounded. There is no distinction between them. The grounded is its own ground. For example if 'X' is the ground of 'Y' and 'Y' is the grounded of 'X', the ground arises as the unity of positive and negative, in which each side is grounded in the other. Hence 'X' is the ground of 'Y' and 'Y' is equally the ground of 'X'. 'X' is grounded on 'Y' and 'Y' is equally grounded on 'X'. Hegel holds that this is equivalent to say that 'X' is grounded on 'X' and 'Y' is grounded 'Y'. The grounded is its own ground and vice versa. They are identical and the mediation between them disappears. However, the grounded is immediate and the

18. Hegel, *The Science of Logic*, Op. cit., pp. 445-46

ground is mediate. Hegel calls the grounded which is immediately present as 'there' existence.[19] Since the grounded is dependent on the ground, ground is regarded as another existent. Since, the ground and the grounded determine each other, we have a number of existences which reciprocally determine each other, as ground and grounded.

The category of existence passes to the category of thing. As already mentioned, the relation of self-to-self is ground, whereas the relation of self-to-other is grounded. The unity of ground and grounded is existence. Existence consists both sides of the relation. Hegel equates the relation of self-to-self with reflection-into-self and self-to-other with reflection into another. Every existent contains these two factors. The reflection-into-self means a stable and self identical being which is independent of other existents; it is what it is and altogether, apart from others. The reflection-into-another means that the existent is dependent on the others. The existent, regarded in this dual aspect, is called a thing. The reflection-into-other speaks of the thing's relation to the other things which have properties. Property has no existence apart from the thing but it is not identical with the thing. Property is reflection-into-another. It speaks of a thing's influence on other things and also its capacity of being influenced by them. For example, water rusts iron. It is the property of water that it influences iron. It is also a property of iron to be influenced by water. This mutual or reflective relation, of reflection-into-other is called the category of thing and its properties which passes to the thing and matter.[20] As already mentioned, property is dependent on the thing. Yet the property and the thing are not the same. Property can also

19. Wallace, William, Loc. cit., p. 230
20. Ibid., pp. 232-34

be regarded as having an independent being. There can be no thing without properties which could be as self-identical as the thing itself. The thing is made of the properties which are not regarded as inhering in the thing. The properties are materials which constitute the thing. These materials are called by Hegel 'matters'. Hegel says, "The properties are not merely different from each other; they are also self-identical, independent, and relieved from their attachment to the thing. Still, as they are the characters of the thing distinguished from one another (as reflected-into-self), they are not themselves things, if things be concrete; but only existences reflected into themselves as abstract characters. They are what are called matters."[21] Hegel considers magnetism and heat properties which are not things but semi-independent entities. Now, the Idea proceeds dialectically to matter and form.

Matters are many and they are different from one another. Each is abstract identity without difference. There is no distinction between them. So matter is one. It is featureless, characterless and undetermined. The thing is constituted by matters. But unlike matter, the thing is of distinction and determination. It is excluded from the matter. So the matter is reflection-into-self whereas the thing is reflection-into-another. Hegel calls the thing with all distinctions form. Form imposes character, definition and determination upon the indeterminate matter.[22] According to Hegel, matter is not a formed material like iron or lead or water but a boundless, indefinite and formless substrate of things. Form is not merely shape; it is the totality of determinations and a principle of differentiation by which matter is defined as a particular thing. The category of matter

21. Wallace, William, Loc. cit., p. 234
22. Ibid., p. 236

and form marks the end of the category of the essence as the ground of existence. Now, the idea passes to the category of appearance, the antithesis of the essence as ground of existence.

(ii) *Appearance* : As it is already observed, a thing or an existence is both matter and form. As matter, it is an existence in reflection-into-self and as form, it is reflection-into-another, Thus an existence is contradiction. That is, an existence is both independent and dependent˙ It is independent in terms of reflection-into-self and dependent in terms of reflection-into-another. Thus an existence repudiates its independence and annuls itself and terms out to be dependent. And appearance is existence conceived as a dependent 'entity'.[23] Hegel holds that appearance is not a mere nullity or unreality. It is as much real as the essence of the existence. Essence and appearance are not two things but one. They are the same thing put twice, once as essence and again as appearance. Indeed, appearance is the essence itself which appears.* Appearance has three phases, viz., (1) the world of appearance, (2) content and form, and (3) relation or correlation.

The transition from appearance to the world of appearance is as follows. As mentioned above, this is the composition of matter and form. Matter as reflection-into-self is the inner being or essence of the thing, whereas the form as reflection-into-another, is outer being. Hegel calls form which is appearance, the phenomenon. The phenomenon implies

---

23. Wallace, Willam, Loc. cit., pp. 239-41

* For Hegel the appearance and essence are deeper thought than the common antithesis of appearance and reality. According to this common antithesis, the outer being is illusory while the inner alone is real. This is similar to the concept of Māyā and Brahman in the School of Vedanta, in Indian Philosophy.

phenomena which is matter. Each is dependent on the other. One is part of the other. Each is the ground of the other. A phenomenon has its ground in another phenomenon which has in turn its ground in yet another phenomenon and so on. Thus there is a multiplicity of phenomena which are all linked together. The totality of these phenomena is the 'world of appearance'. Since Hegel's logic deals only with pure thought, the world of appearance is not to be mistaken for the world itself. The 'world' here means phenomenality of the world which is pure thought but not a thing.

The category of the world of appearance passes to the category of content and form. As already mentioned, a thing is both matter and form which are indifferent to each other. That is, matter and form are separate and externally related. They do not completely determine each other. Matter could be regarded as formless and form could be regarded as matterless. But content and form completely determine each other. Content and form are indissolubly fused together. Hegel gives a poem as an example. In poem, it is not possible to separate its content from its form. Each constitutes the other. The change in the one affects the other. Form is not imposed on the content from outside. Form is the inherent part of content.

The category of content and form passes to the category of correlation which contains the following sub-categories, viz., whole and parts, force and its manifestation and inner and outer. Here, each category consists of two sides which are equal, and identical. It may be recalled that even the categories of reflection are of the nature of correlation. They also have two sides. But the mutual dependence between the sides of the categories of correlation is more advanced than that of the categories of reflection In the sphere of correlation, the each side is only the other side under a different aspect.

The relation of whole and parts consists of two things which are equal and indifferent to one another. This is the definition of the relation of 'whole and parts.'[24] This relation is purely mechanical and immediate, since the two are not organically or necessarily connected with each another, as in the case of a heap of wheat consisting of fifteen lumps. The heap may be treated as the whole or as the parts of fifteen lumps of wheat. In this the two terms are identical and equal to one another. The whole is equal to the sum of parts. But yet the relation between whole and parts is one of indifference, for it makes no difference whether the part, namely, the lump of wheat, is a part of whole or stands by itself without being a part. In any case the lump of wheat remains to be so. Same is the case with the whole; a whole may be a whole either by having parts as piled or as scattered. The formation of the parts does not affect the nature of the whole. This relation of unity and plurality between the whole and the parts passes to the category of forces and its manifestation.

As it has been observed, identity and difference are the main categories of Hegel's logic. Hegel represents identity with the concept of reflection-into-self and difference with that of reflection-into-another. They interact with each other. One becomes the other. Reflection-into-self of necessity reveals itself as reflection-into-another. So also reflection-into-another goes back into the reflection-into-self. That is the essence or matter or content does not remain as it is, instead it manifests itself as properties and form. The identity or unity manifests itself in plurality and variety which equally recedes back into the unity. Thus the Idea arrives at the category of force and the manifestation of force wherein the mutual relation between unity and plurality is best expressed. Force of necessity manifests itself in a different way. Force and its manifestation are one and the same. One without the

24. Wallace, William, Loc. cit., p. 245

other is a non-existent. Force without its manifestation is an empty abstraction of reflection-into-self devoid of reflection-into-another which is absurd. The category of force and manifestation of force. like the world of appearance does not stand for any empirical material. The name of the category is only metaphysical. This passes to the category of the inner and outer. As a consequence of the previous category, force can be regarded as inner being and its manifestations as outer being. The one is of identity and the other is of difference. But as regards the content the distinction between force and manifestation disappears and thus we are at the outer and inner which are identical. Here the mediation between the two terms is explicit and then interdependence is complete. Hegel regards the inner being of man as identical with his actions which constitute the outer being. The inner necessarily becomes the outer and vice versa. The category of inner and outer which is the last category of appearance passes to actuality.

(iii) *Actuality*—The deduction of actuality from inner and outer is as follows. Inner is the essence and outer is the appearance. But the inner and outer are identical. So also the essence and appearance are united. Hegel calls this unity actuality. Actuality arises when the distinction between the inner and outer is sublated. Actual, according to Hegel, is what is actualized, fully realized and operative. Actual is that which, atleast in principle, entails individuality, definiteness and a sensuous concreteness of being here and now.[25] Actuality according to Hegel, is necessity. That is, in the actual 'the possibility of necessity becomes the real. It is the force fully expressed in its manifestations. When the appearance which is contingent and possible transforms itself into the real that actuality takes place. It is an immediate being corresponding to the immediate side of the reality wherein conflict between possible and real is overcome. It is the "return" of reality to itself, to its actual state. It is a process of destroying existing forms and replacing them by new ones. It is a process of self-realization which involves self-destruction and self-transcendence.[26] The necessity that operates here is not mechanical but rational. That is, it is not by accident or chance that the possible becomes the actual. If it is said that "the Sultan may become the Pope", here the necessity of its happening involves 'may be' and 'may not be'. It is contingent but not rational and necessary, since external conditions may not allow the Sultan to embrace Christianity."[27] So it is only a probability. Rational necessity involves self-evidence which has its ground in itself. That is, possibility or the given with rational necessity ought or must become its actuality. Thus Hegel declares that all actuality is rationality and vice versa. Rational is reasonable. So the actual is also reasonable. The category of actuality develops itself into substance and accident, cause and effect and reciprocity (action and reaction). Substance is the first phase of actuality. It is nothing but the actuality which is self-grounded and self-determined. Substance is that which has an independent being. Substance is a being of self-relation, identity and unity. As we have already seen, every self-relation is a relation to another. So Substance manifests itself in the diversity of its modifications. Hegel calls these modifications accidents. The substance does not disappear into accidents. Instead, it swallows and includes them into itself. In fact, accidents are only passing modifications of the being of substance. The category of substance and accidents passes to the category of cause and effect. As already mentioned, substance puts forth its accidents and absorbs them back itself. This process involves double negation. First negation is substance manifesting itself in its accidents and second is substance absorbing them into itself. Thus substance negates itself twice.[28] Hegel regards double negation as concrete and

25. Wallace, William, Loc. cit., pp, 257-9
26. Marcuse Herbert, Loc. cit., pp. 151-53
27. Wallace, William, Loc. cit., p. 261.
Ibid., p. 276.

absolute negativity. He regards substance's power of double negation as activity. So we have now the concepts of an active substance which exerts power over its accidents and passive accidents which receive that power. The former is cause and the latter effect. This moves on to another category called reciprocity. The cause and effect are not totally distinct from each other. What is passive is also active. The effect, like the cause, is substance which is absolute negativity. The effect operates on the cause as much as the cause operates on the effect. So effect can be regarded as cause as well. Hegel calls this relationship between cause and effect reciprocity or action and reaction.[29]

The reciprocal interaction is not the ultimate category, since it has its own defects. Reciprocity is only a category in which substance merely uses its varied inter-course with other substances to bring out its own nature. It is a category, in which there is mutual interference among substances. But Hegel aims at arriving a substance in which there is no reciprocity but perfect harmony which is freedom. He says that such a freedom is only imlicit in reciprocity. Therefore, Reason passes towards another important category called Notion, which is the synthesis of Being and Essence and wherein freedom is explicit.

Section C
NOTION

Notion is an important sphere of thought with which Hegel has raised philosophy to the highest standpoint. For Hegel, Notion is not an opinion. It is neither an aberration of speculation nor an arbitrary thinking of an individual. On the contrary, Notion is an inevitable consequence of the dialectical movement of Idea.

---

29. Wallace, William, Loc. cit., p. 280

The German equivalent of Notion is 'Begriff' which is commonly used to mean 'concept'. But Hegel distinguishes Notion from concept. Generally, the generic universals like man, table, goodness etc., are regarded as concepts. Concept is an abstract universal as against the particular which is a concrete reality. It is an empty and an indeterminate universal, purely subjective and devoid of content. The concept can only be 'thought' but cannot be 'realized' as the particular. As against this, Hegel's Notion is a concrete universal containing the particular within itself. The Notion is a universal which involves self-determination. That is, the Notion is the universal determined by the particular. It is the determinate identity of opposites.

Nevertheless, Hegel's Notion can also be regarded as abstract in that it does not occur in experience and reflection. It lacks the spatial and temporal material of the sensuous world. It does not involve the reflective division of the subject and the object. Yet, Notion is not something dead and unreal but the principle of all life. Notion is what is true in things. It is through Notion that an "object is reduced to its non-contingent essential nature."[30] It possesses the character of thorough concreteness, for it contains within itself the total wealth of the categories which constitute the universe.[31]

The Notion is not a presumption but a reality emerging out of the inner dialectic of the Idea. It is a reality produced from its own resources. Its truth is not borrowed but "generated solely by the immanent deduction which contains its genesis and which already lies behind us."[32]

Notion is the synthesis of Being and Essence. As

30. Hegel, *The Science of Logic*, Op. cit., p. 591
31. Wallace, William, Loc. cit., p. 288
32. Hegel, *The Science of Logic*, Op. cit., p. 582

already said, Being the sphere of immediacy and abstract universal. Essence is the sphere of mediacy and empty identity. The Notion is the sphere of self-mediation and absolute unity. As Hegel puts, "Notion is the absolute unity of being and reflection in which being is in and for-itself only in so far as it is no less reflection or positedness is no less being that is in and for-itself."[33]

Notion is a consequence of double negation. Essence is the first negation of Being and Notion is the second negation or the negation of the negation. Yet, in Notion, the Being and Essence do not get annulled but emerge with their true nature. Notion reveals Being and Essence with their true determination. In Notion, Being attains infinite self-mediation and Essence gets liberated from the determination by its opposite. Notion is the unconditioned positedness and "the liberated manifestation of essence."[34]

Hegel regards substance the governing sub-category of Essence as the immediate genesis of Notion. Substance is the proximate presupposition of Notion. Notion is the explicit manifestation of what is implicit in substance. "Notion is the truth of substance"[35] revealed through the dialectical movement of substance through its sub-categories of causality and reciprocity. Now let us briefly consider the chief moments of the dialectic movement of substance. As already mentioned, substance is both reflection-into-itself and the other. That is, substance in being itself, of necessity posits itself as the other which is none other than its accidents. Thus substance manifests itself as accidentality. But the truth is that the accidentality is not different from the substance. Accidentality is what the substance has put forth itself in its other. So accidentality is also a substance. It is as 'real' as the substance itself. So there are two substances. The

33. Hegel, *The Science of Logic*, Op. cit., p. 577
34. Ibid., p. 591
35. Ibid., p. 577

first substance acts on the second one. Now the relation between them is causality. The first one acts as the cause of the other which is passive and therefore called effect. But the second one is equally a substance. So the effect also acts on the cause. The effect is a cause which is not passive but a reaction on the first substance. Now the relation of substance to itself is one of reciprocity wherein the two substances, cause and effect are identical. Thus, the substance in passing into its opposite, passes only into itself, for the substance is in absolute identity with itself. And Notion is the totality resulting from the reciprocal relation of substance wherein the difference between the two substances revealed as having the status of an illusory being. In notion, the mutual opacity of substances standing in the causal relationship has vanished and become a self-transparent clarity. Thus the substance gets raised to the status of Notion which, Hegel calls the subject.[36]

Hegel attributes self-consciousness to the subject with self-consciousness, for it is totally aware of itself as it ought to be. He also attributes freedom to the subject, since it has negated all its contingencies. It is the knowledge of truth in the sense that it is the what *is* of everything. It unveils the real nature of 'being' as realised by a knowing subject. Notion, being self-transparent, has the character of 'immediacy' which is not of being. It is immediacy that has made itself immediate through the sublation of mediacy.[37]

As already said, Notion is the substance transformed into the subject. In other words, Notion is the exposition of substance as subject which alone comprehends the objectivity of an object. Intuition and reflection of Being and Essence cannot grasp the real worth and status of the objectivity of the object. Thought the governing principle of subject, alone can comprehend the objectivity by 'treating' the object not as external

36. Hegel, *The Science of Logic*, Op. cit., p. 582
37. Marcuse, Herbert, Loc. cit., pp. 153-55

and alien but truly in and for-itself. Objectivity is the unity of thought into which the object has been received. Notion is the objectivity which is the same as thought or self-consciousness which has the 'I' as its determination. Thus Hegel defines notion as a purely "abstract" universality which includes specific determinateness. Notion contains within itself absolute determinateness and individuality. In fact it is the ground of all finite determinateness and manifoldness of the external world.[38]

Let us now deal with the development of Notion towards the Absolute Idea through its various sub-categories possessing the character of self-mediation.

Notion develops itself through three stages, namely 1. subjective notion, 2. objective notion and 3. Idea.

(i) *Subjective Notion*—Subjetive notion is the Notion which is in itself. In is the truth which is implicit. It is subjective thinking which is in relation only with itself. Hegel calls it subjectivity or formal Notion.[39] It is divided into 1. the notion as notion, 2. the judgment and 3. the syllogism. Notion as notion has three factors within itself, namely, the universal, the particular and the singular or individual. The universal is the absolute identity of opposites. It is concrete in the sense that it contains the particular within itself. That is, the notion as universal opposes itself by the particular which is itself. This duality does not last long but gets negated soon again. Now there is the absolute identity and difference which results in the third factor, namely, the individual. The notion as individual involves an absolute self-determined unity. The three moments constitute the whole of notion as notion which involves the double negation of notion going forth into its opposite and again returning into itself.[40]

---

38. Hegel, *The Science of Logic*, Op. cit., p. 589.
39. Ibid., p. 596.
40. Stace, W. T., Loc. cit., pp. 227-28

Now the Idea passes from notion as notion to judgment. The judgment issues from the individual, the last category of the notion as notion. The individual is the identity and the totality of the universal and the particular which are equally independent totalities. As the Notion moves further, its unity suffers from diremption into the three independent totalities. It is this diremption of the unity of the Notion into independent moments that Hegel calls the judgment. Judgment is an expression of self-determinism of notion by itself. Hegel calls judgment "the proximate realization of the Notion, in as much as reality denotes in general entry into existence as a determinate being."[41] Judgment contains the two self-substances, viz., subject and predicate which are indeterminate by themselves and essentially independent totalities. Judgment is the reflection that unites them as this or that. As Hegel puts it, "The judgment is the self-diremption of the Notion;........ It is thus the original division (Teilung) of what is originally one."[42]

Judgment passes through four phases, viz., 1. The judgment of existence, 2. the judgment of reflection, 3. the judgment of necessity, and 4. the judgment of the notion. The judgment of existence is the judgment of immediacy. It is a positive judgment in which the subject is an abstract individual which simply is and the predicate is an abstract universal which is a determinateness of the subject. Hegel says that the judgment of existence can also be called the qualitative judgment.[43] It affirms an identity between an individual and universal. For example, this rose is red. The judgment becomes defective when it is reversed. The defect lies in the inadequacy of the relation between the subject and predicate. The predicate is of wider scope and therefore does not

---

41. Hegel, *The Science af Logic*, Op. cit., p. 623.
42. Ibid., p. 625
43. Ibid., pp. 630-31

correspond to the subject. It applies to countless other things besides the subject. To overcome this defect Hegel passes to the negative judgment. The positive judgment relates the subject with the predicate. It merely enunciates that the subject is predicate or the individual is the universal and vice versa. Its content is purely logical. So it is not true. Hegel says by virtue of this purely logical content, the positive judgment is not true, but has its truth in the negative judgment. In negative judgment the disparity between individual and universal is not abstractly universal. In it, the subject will be an individual object and the predicate will be some universal which has absolutely no connection and compatibility with the subject. Eg., 'rose' is not an 'elephant' or the 'tiger' is not a 'chair'. However, Hegel treats these judgments as meaningless, for it is not clear as what their nature really is. He says, "These judgments are correct or true, as the expression goes, but inspite of such truth they are nonsensical and absurd."[44] So it passes on to the judgment of reflection. In judgment of reflection the predicates are essentialities, which relate objects to other objects. In it, the development will be on the part of subject but not of predicate. "They express an essential determination, but one which is in a relationship or is a unifying universality."[45] Eg., "This house is useful." Hegel calls it a singular judgment which is not adequate because it contains only a singular subject to the essential predicate. So Hegel passes on to particular judgment like "some house is useful." It is also not adequate but better in comparison with the earlier. Hence Hegel passes to the universal judgment, like "All houses are useful." It involves a merely enumerative universality that can never be completed. What it says is valid only subject to the provision that particular instances shall not be approached. This inadequacy

44. Hegel, *The Science of Logic*, Op. cit., p. 642
45. Ibid., p. 643

can be cured by passing on to the 'judgment of necessity' wherein the subject is species and the predicate is a genus. The first phase of this judgment is called categorical judgment, e.g., "the rose is a plant." In it the specific concept connects the general one, which is a part of its content, for instance, 'being a plant.' Hegal contends that these categorical judgments too are inadequate because they veil the necessity, which is inwardly implied. So he passes over to hypothetical judgment, like 'if that is hellobore, it will kill you.' In it, necessity is explicit, for the ground of hypothetical judgment will always be of some specific nature carrying with it some generic nature which necessarily carries its features into every possible specification. But this ground may not be fully explicit. There are many 'broken backed' hypothetical judgments in which the connection between antecedent and consequent does not seem to be necessary.[46] This inadequacy is remedied in disjunctive judgment like 'A' must by its nature be either 'B' or 'C'. In it, the same genus or universal appears to be both as 'subject' and 'predicate.' At times it appears in its pervasive universality and at other times in the totality of its 'specifications.' In it there is the accurate identity between the subject and the predicate which is Notion. And Notion is nothing but this identity or unity of the subject (particular) and the predicate (universal).

The disjunctive judgment, though exhibits the identity of the universal and the particular, fails to show the universal as its being not only in the particular but also in the individual. The universal predicate has yet to be shown as being absolutely identical with the individual subject. Thus arises the judgment of notion wherein the individual subject and a universal predicate are absolutely identical. For example, "Man is not rational." This speaks of the essential universal nature of man which is reason. It tells us whether a man is truly man. A man may be snub nosed or not. It is irrelevant

46. Hegel, *The Science of Logic*, Op. cit., p. 653

to his manhood. But the absence of rationality destroys manhood. This statement, "This man is rational" is the same as "This man is a man." "This man" (individual) is absolutely identical with "a man" (universal) though they are different as individual and universal.

The judgment of notion appears in three forms : 1. the assertory judgment, 2. the problematic judgment, and 3. the apodictic judgment. The assertory judgment states the agreement or disagreement of the individual subject with universal predicate as when we say that 'this rose is fragrant' or 'this rose is not fragrant'. This judgmant also gives reasons for the conformity or non-conformity of the subject and predicate. It states that this house (individual) is good or not good (universal) because it is thus and thus constructed (singular) or this house must not be good because it is not thus and thus constructed.[47] The problematic judgment is that which expresses doubt over the assertory ones which merely assert or negate the predicate to the subject. They are mere opinions. Thus they give rise to problematic judgments like this picture may (or may not) be beautiful. The problematic judgment, being doubtful and contingent, leads us to the apodictic judgment.

The apodictic judgment exhibits the absolute identity of the individual and the universal through the particular. It makes the oneness of subject and predicate explicit. Notion is precisely the unity of universal and individual brought about by the particular. Here the particular resembles the middle term of the syllogism. It intermediates the subject and predicate or the individual and the universal. Thus the apodictic judgment gives rise to syllogism.

---

47. Wallace, William, Loc. cit., pp. 312-13
48. Stace, W.T., Loc. cit., p. 247

The syllogism is the synthesis of notion as notion, the thesis and the judgment, the antithesis. In the notion as notion the moments of universal and individual were found "in a primitive and as yet undifferentiated unity."[48] In the judgment the universal and the particular are differentiated into diversity. In the syllogism, the diversity of the universal and the individual is preserved in their unity brought about by the middle term, namely, the particular.

Hegel describes the syllogism as the reasonable. It is the better form of reason than judgment, the product of understanding. He also says that everything in its reality is reasonable and therefore syllogism, since the real is reasonable. Even God is rational only because He is a syllogism in the sense that He involves the Trinity of God, as Father, the Son and the Spirit.[49]

The syllogism, like judgment, manifests itself in three phases, viz., 1. the qualitative syllogism, 2. the syllogism of reflection and 3. the syllogism of necessity. The qualitative syllogism comprises four figures. In the traditional logic, figure I is of the form in which the middle term is the subject in the major premise and predicate in the minor premise. It is of the form viz.,

M—P
S—M
———
S—P
———

According to Hegel, the first figure is of the form viz.,

49. Wallace, William, Loc. cit., p. 317

P—U
S—P

S—U

That is, in figure I, the middle term is the particular (P), the major term is the universal (U) and the minor term is the individual or singular (S).* In it, the middle term (P) mediates the universal and the singular. That is, the universal and the singular find their identity through the particular. So Hegel expresses it as : S—P—U. It could be illustrated as follows :

Green is pleasant.
This fruit is green.
This fruit is pleasant.

Hegel's objection to this figure is that its middle term viz., "green" does not possess the character of necessity. Being "green" cannot be an essential reason for the fruit being pleasant. The middle term is an arbitrary quality which merely *happens* to inhere in the singular. It is a matter of chance that "green" is taken as the middle term. Therefore, it is quite possible to choose any other term, say, "poisonous" as the middle term and derive an opposite conclusion.

Hegel, therefore, contends that the procedure in figure I is not rational, but capricious. It does not exhibit necessary relation between its terms. The middle term "green" and the major term "pleasant" are not necessarily related but arbitrarily asserted. As Hegel puts it, "It is justly held that there

* Hegel calls the minor term either "individual" or "singular". For him, "individual" and "singular" are synonymous. He uses them interchangeably.

is nothing so inadequate as a formal syllogism of this kind, since it is a matter of chance or caprice which middle term is employed."[50]

As mentioned above, the middle term in figure I possesses only a chance character; its position is not one of necessity; it can be replaced by any other term. So Hegel holds that the middle term in figure I is singular or individual only but not particular as it is generally understood.* Therefore, the so called truth of figure I, according to Hegel, can be better expressed by treating the middle term not as particular (which it is not) but as singular (which it is in fact) as is the case in figure II. Thus, figure I gives rise to figure II such as : (P—S—U) :

This fruit is pleasant.
This fruit is green.
Green is pleasant.

It can be expressed symbolically as :

S is U
S is P
———
P is U
———

Figure II** remedies the defect of figure I by deducing

50. Hegel, *The Science of Logic*, Op. cit., p. 671.

* The particular, according to Hegel, is that which is necessarily related to the universal while the singular is that which is arbitrarily brought into connection with the universal by the subjective effort.

** The Hegelian second figure is not the second but the third figure of traditional logic. He has not strictly followed the order and aim of traditional logic. For him, the primary aim of syllogism is to establish the necessary relationship between the terms. For him, real syllogism is that in which universal is united with the individual through the particular. (Hegel, The Science of Logic, Op. cit., p. 669).

as its conclusion the major premise of figure I. Thus, the terms viz., "green" and "pleasant" which were unmediated in figure I get mediated in the conclusion of figure II. However, Hegel contends that even the terms of figure II are not necessarily related but are immediate contingencies only. Its truth consists not in its necessity but in its subjective connection of its terms. Its middle term is not particular but only an individual; the major and minor terms are only random adjectives of the middle term. The truth of its conclusion is not deduced out of necessity but only asserted as a fact. As Hegel puts it, "If the conclusion in the second figure is correct, then it is so because it is so on its own account, not because it is the conclusion of the syllogism."[51]

When compared to figure I, figure II is more adequate, since its conclusion, viz., "Green is pleasant" as well as its major premise viz., "This fruit is pleasant" (being the conclusion of figure I) is mediated. But the defect of figure II is that its minor premise is not yet mediated. This can be remedied in figure III. Thus, figure II passes on to figure III such as (S—U—P) :

Green is pleasant.
This fruit is pleasant.
This fruit is green.

It can be symbolically represented as :

P—U
S—U
———
S—P
———

Here, the minor premise of figure II gets mediated by being deduced as the conclusion. Thus figure III remedies

51. *The Science of Logic*, Op. cit., p. 676

the defect of the unmediated minor premise in the figure II. But, it suffers from the 'fallacy of undistributed middle' which can be remedied if only one of its premises and thereby its conclusion are made negative which is possible in figure IV. Thus figure III* gives rise to figure IV, viz.,

A=B
B=C

A=C

However, Hegel repudiates figure IV** as no figure at all since it is merely the reverse of figure I. The middle term is not necessarily related to the other two terms. As in the case of figure I, the terms in figure IV are purely indifferent

---

* Hegel maintains that the determinations of syllogism get completed with figure III itself. That is, the change of the position of the middle term as particular, individual and universal in three figures respectively comes to an end with figure III itself. Moreover, unlike traditional logic wherein everything is contingent, the determination of the position of the middle term and the sequence of figures in Hegelian logic are dialectical in the sense that the latter is a necessary consequence of the inadequacy of the former. (Hegel, The Science of Logic, Op. cit., p. 678).

** It is held that figure IV of traditional logic does not form part of original Aristotelian logic. It is only a later addition. So Hegel, like Kant, rejects it as superfluous. He holds that it is concerned with pointless and empty distinctions. (See Hegel, The Science of Logic, Op. cit., p. 679.

to each other. Their relation is one of mathematical* equality and external unity; it is absolutely devoid of determination. It is a syllogism which is without comprehension and mediation.[52]

In it all distinctions between extremes and middle term vanish. The universal is connected with the universal by way of the universal. The connections between its terms are like mathematical equations. So it is otherwise called mathematical syllogism. Hegel holds that the mathematical syllogism represents a degenerated form of syllogism. So it passes on to the syllogism of reflection. The first step in syllogism of reflection is syllogism of allness or complete enumeration. For example :

All men are mortal.
Rama is a man.
Rama is mortal.

This too is inadequate, since its major premise bags the question and assumes the truth of its conclusion. It requires the enumeration of all individuals to show the universal. This is humanly impossible. Hence, this 'allness' is a mere pretence of a syllogism. Thus the syllogism of allness passes to the inductive syllogism. This is expressed symbolically as follows :

---

* Hegel calls figure IV mathematical syllogism, since it expresses the indifference of the terms to each other as merely mathematical equality. It neglects the qualitative difference between the terms. Hegel calls it false where the quantitative syllogism is also.

52. Hegel, *The Science of Logic* Op. cit., p. 680

I
S—I—U
I

Hegel contends that it is not an inference but has only an appearance of inference. In it, enumeration of the individuals concerned results in the bad infinite and leaves its conclusion problematic. The 'truth' of inductive syllogism, according to Hegel, is the syllogism of analogy. It reasons from particulars to particulars. It proceeds from certain universal features common to a set of individuals to certain specific features known to be present in some of them. This can be expressed as :

The earth is inhabited.
The moon is an earth.
Moon is inhabited.

Here though the argument is valid, the conclusion is wholly absurd. Its middle term is still a singular. It does not 'represent' the 'all' earths which again meets the defect of complete enumeration which is impossible. Thus it passes on to the syllogism of necessity wherein the middle term is out and out universal. The first kind of the syllogism of necessity is the categorical syllogism. For example :

Man is rational
Socrates is a man
He is rational.

This too is not adequate, since its minor term represents an individual arbitrarily selected. The two extremes of the syllogism have many irrelevant aspects to the middle. So it passes to 'hypothetical syllogism' like 'If A then B, but A, therefore B. The defect of the hypothetical syllogism is that its middle term A is only a fact which is an immediacy. It treats the individual and the species as the genus. It identifies (being) man with being rational (genus). It ignores the fact that the genus is identical with all its species taken together but not with one of them alone. This defect is rectified in the disjunctive syllogism like :

A is either B or C or D.
But A is not B and C.
A is D.

Here the middle term is the universal distributed into its species. It is completely developed into particularity and singularity. It is no longer abstract. It is the concrete totality of the Notion. It exhibits the double negation resulting in immediacy. In the notion as notion, the factors of the Notion are of immediacy. In judgment, the factors fall asunder by mediation. The syllogism shows their mediation of returning to unity. This unity is again an immediacy which is the object. Hegel says that an object is an independent and real individual which is thought of as being penetrated with universal and specific meanings. Thus the middle term of the disjunctive syllogism transforms the subjective notion into the objective notion. Now, the Notion which at first subjective, without the assistance of any foreign stuff and out of its inner necessity "breaks through its own barriers and opens out into objectivity by means of the syllogism."[53] In Notion, the antithesis of subjectivity and objectivity is not rigid, abstract and processless but "wholly dialectical" in the sense that each passes into the other.[54]

The syllogistic process involves the negation of the categories through which it passes: it is a mediative process through which the subject is 'coupled' with itself. The

53. Wallace, William, Loc. cit., p. 329
54. Ibid., p. 335

syllogism is self-mediation or the self-realization of the Notion by itself. Hegel calls the Notion as self-mediation of the object.

He says that an object is a real individual which is thought of as being penetrated with universal and specific meanings. Thus the middle term of the disjunctive syllogism transforms the subjective notion into the objective notion.

(ii) *The Objective Notion* : According to Hegel, the object is something independent, concrete and self-complete. It is the totality of the notion which is itself and still unspecified. This is called the objective as a whole. Hegel terms it as Absolute Object or God. At the same time, the object has parts within itself; it falls into a multiplicity of pieces which are individualistic and therefore objects by themselves. Thus the object is an inherently universal unity containing real distructions as totalities. The object is immediate being which is "the absolute contradiction between a complete independence of the multiplicity, and the equally complete non-independence of the different pieces."[55]

The objectivity comprises the three forms viz., mechanism, chemism and teleology. Mechanism is of three forms : 1. formal mechanism, 2. mechanism with affinity, and 3. absolute mechanism. The formal mechanism is found in the unity of different objects. Here the relation between objects is external and does not touch their inner nature. Truly mechanical objects will be as much 'heaps' or mere aggregates, as the wholes they compose. They cannot exhibit any behaviour of their own. Instead, their behaviour is determined by the behaviour of other objects within or outside of them. Hegel is of the view that the mechanical objects are less and

---

55. Wallace, William, Loc cit., p. 334.

less applicable to the phenomena like light, heat, magnetism and electricity. They are also 'quite' inapplicable to the characteristic performances of life and mind.[56] Mechanical object passes to mechanical process wherein the contradiction is explicit. In the mechanical process the object is connected with other objects by its inner nature. So Hegel calls this category mechanism with affinity. In it, the objects show themselves to be not really indifferent to one another but communicate and influence without doing violence to one another. Under this category, Hegel deals with transmission of motion, electricity, magnetism etc. However, Hegel recognizes conflict that arises when a mechanical object resists some influence communicated by another object. The resistance is overcome in another category called the absolute mechanism.

In absolute mechanism the relation between the objects is purely external but not indifferent to their inner nature. Here the inner nature of the object is what it is in and through the other object. That is, the being of an object is the being of the other. The inner nature of the objects coalesce into one another without resistance. Chemism is precisely the identity of the inner nature of the objects. In chemism, Hegel deals with chemical objects and the process of chemical combinations of elements. In chemism, Hegel uses the language of syllogism to cover the facts of chemical union. In a chemical union major and minor terms are brought together by a middle term. The result of this is a neutral product. In neutral product the properties of two extremes are cancelled for time being, The middle term is the inner nature of the two chemical substances. It reveals

56. Wallace, William, Loc. cit., p. 347.

their common concept in their mutual affiinity. Hegel takes water or air as the medium or the middle term in the chemical sphere.

Chemism has two sides, viz., chemical union and separation. They are identical in the sense that the chemically isolated elements cannot isolate or unite themselves. In both cases external conditions and provocations are needed to reverse the process. To overcome this defect chemism passes to teleology. In chemism the notion emerges from the world of objects. In teleology, the notion negates the world and enters an independent and free existence of its own, like a soul which has escaped from the body in which it was imprisoned.[57]

Teleology is the synthesis of mechanism and chemism. It involves the self-contained totality of the mechanical object and the principle of differentiation of chemism.[58] Teleology which is constituted by ends and means, is in fact deduced from chemism which is the unity of plurality of objects. The unity is the end and the factor of plurality is the means. Teleology is of two types : (1) external design, (2) inner design. In the former, the means and end are quite different and independent. For example, money may be used as means of obtaining bread. The money as means and bread as end are quite distinct from each other. Hegel calls this the finite form of teleology. In the latter, the end and means are identical. One cannot exist without the other. For example, the living organism and its parts are the means which exist for the sake of the whole. The whole and the parts or the end and the means are not distinct. This Hegel considers the true teleology which has (1) the subjective end, (2) the

57. Stace, W. T., Loc. cit., p. 237
58. Wallace, William, Loc. cit., p. 336

means, and (3) the realized end as its categories. The subjective end is a mere ideal and not yet objectified itself. The means is the purposive action which relates the idea and the object. It annuls the gap between the ideal and the object. The result is the realized end. Now the end ceases to be subjective and becomes objective. Thus in teleology the notion translates itself into objectivity. "The teleological process is the translation of the Notion that has a distinct concrete existence as Notion into objectivity."[59]

(iii) *The Idea* : We have so far seen the Notion as subjectivity as well as objectivity. The Notion as subject is the thesis and as the object the antithesis. The synthesis is the Idea which is the unity of the subject and the object. The Notion as subject is the reality in-itself and the Notion as object is the reality in-its otherness and the Idea is the reality in and for-itself.

Let us now see the transition from teleology to the Idea. Teleology has the realized end as its final category in which the means and end are united. The means constitute the factor of plurality and the end the whole. For example, an organism or a whole is constituted by many separate parts which are the means of the organism. Here the plurality of parts is not different from the organism. The organism along with its parts is a single whole. It is at times viewed as the plurality of its parts and as a unity at some other times.

Now the factor of plurality or the means is the objectivity and the factor of unity or the end is the subjectivity. Therefore the unity of the end and means is nothing but the

---

59. Hegel, *The Science of Logic*, Op. cit., p. 747

unity of the subject and the object. The Idea is precisely this identity of the subject and the object. The Idea is the realization or explicit manifestation of the implicit unity of the subject and the object of the realised end.[60] The Idea implies that the universe is of the nature of thought in which the abstraction of the subject and the separation of the object are annulled. The universe is neither simply subject nor simply object. It is the Idea which is both in one. The Idea is truth in which there is the absolute correspondence* of objectivity with the notion as subjectivity.[61]

The idea is the dialectical process which, for ever, in its unity, divides the subjective from the objective, the finite from the infinite, the soul from the body and the self-identical from the differentiated. The Idea passes through three stages namely (1) life, (2) knowledge or congnition, and (3) the Absolute Idea.

Life** is the pure Idea in its immediacy. It is purely logical which is devoid of unphilosophical and scientific

---

60. Wallace, William, Loc. cit., p. 351

61. Ibid., p. 352

* The correspondence of the Idea is not the same as that between the external things and the conceptions of an individual person. The correspondence of the latter is correct only as held by a particular person. In Idea, the individual, the external object and the conception do not matter. The correspondence of the Idea implies that everything actual is the Idea. Everything has its truth in and by virtue of the Idea alone.

** The category of life does not imply consciousness. Hegel takes plants rather than animals as examples of the category of life. The term life is rather to be taken metaphorically than literally.

presuppositions. "Life, in the Idea, is without such presuppositions which are in the form of shapes of actuality its presupposition is the Notion as we have considered it, on the one hand as subjective, on the other hand as objective."[62] Life as the Idea is an absolute universality which is in and for itself. It possesses within itself the whole Notion as its omnipresent soul which outpours itself into the multiplicity of objective being. The soul is both a simple self relation and the complexity of self externality. It is the unity of the oneness of subjectivity and the multiplicity of objectivity. Hegel describes this immediate and simple life as an absolute contradiction and an "incomprehensible mystery for which understanding is of no avail."[63]

The category of life manifests itself in three phases, namely, 1. the living individual, 2. the life-process, and 3. the genus process or the process of kind. Life as the living individual is the subjective totality which existing for itself indifferently to an objectivity which confronts it as indifferent. It is a self-determining particular which is of the creative universal soul. It is the subject which reproduces itself in the threefold from of sensibility, irritability and reproduction. As sensibility, the living individual is immediately simple self-relation and the soul that is omnipresent in the body. As irritability, it appears split up in itself. And as reproduction, it is a continually self-renewing process within its own limits.[64]

In the life-process, the living individual assimilates its external objectivity and attains the character of reality to itself. Here, life as immediacy is mediated by its external objectivity and thus becomes the process of kind.

---

62. Hegel, *The Science of Logic,* Op. cit., 726.
63. Ibid., p. 763
64. Wallace, William, Loc. cit., p, 360

The process of kind is the unity of the subject and the object or the organic and the inorganic. The living being stands in a negative attitude towards the process of kind. The process of kind is the essential universality and a superior power in which the individual sinks. "In the process of kind, the immediate living being mediates itself with itself and rises above its immediacy, only however to sink back into it again."[65]

Thus the Idea of life through its three stages overcomes its immediacy and becomes freely self-conscious. It enters upon the existence which is free and self-subsistent. Hegel calls this the knowledge or the cognition.

In the category of kind, organism is universal which assimilates the inorganic into itself. The inorganic can also be external world confronting the organism in the form of the living individual. But the external world is not only outside the individual but also within the individual. The external world has proceeded from the organism only. And cognition is nothing but the fact that the individual cognizes the world not only because the world is there external to him but also because the world appeals within the consciousness of the individual. Therefore, cognition is the unity of the subject and the object. Cognition is also consciousness wherein the external world becomes internal to the subject. Cognition has two sub-categories,* namely, cognition proper and volition. In cognition proper the subject passively receives the external world into itself. In it, the object modifies the subject. Its aim is to grasp the world as it is. Hegel also calls it the theoretical Idea. Hegel calls it finite cognition, since it still involves the division or separation between the subject and

---

65. Wallace, William, Loc. cit., p. 362

* Here the deduction is not triadic. Hegel abandons the triadic method.

the world. The finite cognition comprises two methods, viz., analytic and synthetic. The analytic method begins with the individual and ends with the universal. It can also be called the method of induction. The synthetic method proceeds from the universal and descends through demonstration to the less general or individual. The analytic method analyses the given concrete object and isolates its differences and gives them the form of abstract universality.[66] The synthetic method starts with the universal as a definition; proceeds through the particular (in division) to the individual (the theorm).[67] In volition, the subject is regarded as active. It moulds the world and conforms it to the subject. Unlike cognition proper, notion is the principle of action by the will of the subject. It is with the volition that the theoretical idea passes to the practical idea in which the volition as will aims at the idea of the good. The idea of the good is superior to the idea of cognition, "for it possesses not only the worth of the universal but also of the out-and-out actual."[68] The good is universal, for it is valid in and for-itself; it is actual for it is an action to some particular end, which is true on its own account as well as through its realization. Hegel says, that the realized good is good by virtue of what it already is in its Idea; realization only gives good and external existence which is intrinsically worthless. It renders good contingent restricted and destructible. It makes good relative and creates the conflict of the good itself by bringing about several kinds of good. Hegel says that "the very realization of the good is exposed to obstacles, obstacles which may indeed even be insurmountable."[69]

---

66. Wallace, William, Loc. cit., p. 365
67. Ibid., p. 366
68. Hegel, *The Science of Logic*, Op. cit., pp. 818-19
69. Ibid., p. 820

Thus the category of good remains as an ought to-be in and for-itself on the one side and the realized good remains as an absolute postulate on the other. "There are still two worlds in opposition, one a realm of subjectivity in the pure regions of transparent thought, the other realm of objectivity in the element of an externally manifold actuality that is an undisclosed realm of darkness."[70]

Thus the Idea of the good and the realized good still remain in an unresolved contradiction. The realized good does not correspond to its Idea. Hegel says, "It is only the will itself that stands in the way of the attainment of its goal, for it separates itself from cognition and the external reality for the will does not receive the form of a true being"[71]

The Idea of the good finds its integration only in the Idea of the true. Wherein the cognition which is free and universal self-identity is united with the practical Idea, which is actuality not only as given but also as determined and realized absolute end. Now, the subject knows the object as immediately as it knows itself. The subject knows the objectivity no less truly than the subject knows itself as the notion that is determined in and for-itself. The objectivity or the actuality appears as an objective world whose inner ground and actual subsistence is the notion. Hegel calls this the Absolute Idea.[72]

Hegel describes the Absolute Idea as rational notion which in its reality meets with itself. It is pure thought which alone is true and in which difference is not otherness. It is perfectly transparent to itself. It is self-determination of apprehending itself. Hegel says, "All else is error, confusion,

---

70. Hegel, *The Science of Logic*, Op. cit., p. 820.
71. Ibid., p. 821
72. Ibid., p. 823

opinion, endeavour, caprice and transitariness; the Absolute Idea alone is being, imperishable life, self-knowing truth, and is all truth."[73]

The Absolute Idea is the unity and the truth of the theoretical and the practical ideas. It is both in itself and for-itself. It is its own object. It is for-itself and the pure form of notion, which contemplates its content as its own self. It is the unity of form and content. It is its own content and also the totality of the determinations which describes its content. The content of the Absolute Idea, according to Hegel, is the content of the entire system of Logic. It is not an empty abstraction but an absolute and universal form into which the entire content of all the categories has retired. It is an embodiment of the whole content it has brought into being through the dialectical movement. Thus the being which begins to evolve in the realm of being has now attained the stage of Absolute Idea. The movement of Idea or Reason from being to Absolute Idea implies the comprehension of the entire content which it has passed through. The content of the Absolute Idea is not an invention but the 'speculation' of what had already been there. It is the living development of the Idea itself. Hegel compares the Absolute Idea to a matured man for whom an utterance has quite a different meaning from that of a child. Hegel says, "The absolute idea may in this respect be compared to the old man who utters the same creed as the child, but for whom it is pregnant with the significance of a life time. Even if the child understands the truths of religion, he cannot but imagine them to be something outside of which lies the whole of life and the whole of the world."[74]

---

73. Hegel, *The Science of Logic*, Op. cit., p. 824
74. Wallace, William, Loc. cit., p. 375

Thus the Idea passing through Being, Essence and Notion attains the stage of the Absolute. Being exhibits Idea as what it is in its immediacy. Essence shows it as what it is in its immediacy sublated by mediation. Being evolves through various stages by the dialectical force immanent in it. Now the Idea, being pure does not require to evolve further to a higher category. The Idea stands for absolute liberation which needs no more determination.[75]

Nevertheless, the Absolute Idea which is so far enclosed within pure thought of Logic has the urge to sublate its 'abstract subjectivity'. So it goes forth, freely as Nature. Nature is only the 'other-being' of the Idea. It is the reflected image of the Idea itself. It is the externalization of the idea but not its extension. Thus we pass from Logic of Nature which we are going to consider in the ensuing chapter.

75. Hegel, *The Science of Logic,* Op. cit., p. 843

CHAPTER III

DIALECTIC IN HEGEL'S PHILOSOPHY OF NATURE

Introduction

As we have seen in the previous chapter, the Idea having been completely liberated from all its imperfections and inadequacies, attains the status of the Absolute. The Absolute, being fully self-mediated, self-realized and no longer sullied by its opposite, does not transit any more. Thus in Logic, the dialectical movement of the Idea comes to an end with the Absolute Idea which is a pure transparency to itself.

However, the Idea which is pure Reason 'freely decides' to externalize itself in the form of Nature. It lets itself manifest as Nature while remaining certain of itself (the Idea) and tranquil with itself.[1] It releases itself from its 'abstraction' and determines itself as Nature.*

---

1. Findlay, J. N., *Hegel Re-examination*, George Allen and Unwin Ltd., London, 1958, p. 28

* Hegel picturises the Absolute Idea as externalizing itself as Nature, because the Absolute Idea, being God, would be a mere, abstraction if it does not do so. The Idea or God in pure abstraction is a contradiction in terms. Abstract God is not true God. Therefore the Absolute Idea must of necessity externalize itself as Nature. Here Hegel seeks to fulfil the requirement of the 'creation' of the world by treating the Absolute Idea's transition to Nature as necessary, rational and real.

Dialectically speaking, Nature is the antithesis of the thesis, namely, the Idea. Nature is the Idea gone out of itself into its otherness. It is the Idea in its self-estrangement; it is the Idea in its diremption into the finite existents that are external to one another. The Absolute Idea is the universal and the Nature is its specificity (or particularity). The former is rational and necessary while the latter is irrational and contingent. Though antithetical to each other, the Idea and Nature are not absolutely separate and different but pass into each other. They are at once different and identical.

In 'the Philosophy of Nature' Hegel presents a progress of the infinite forms of Nature from lower to higher. In it, he gives a rational justification for the heirarchy of the forms of Nature. Just as Logic consists of the evolution of the cotegories of increasing value, Nature comprises a series of natural forms of increasing value. However, the forms of Nature succeed one another in logical order but not in the order of time. The dialectical evolution of the form of Nature is not historical but rational. Indeed, the development of Nature is in reality the dialectical movement of its inner principle, namely, the Idea. It is the Idea which is the principle of inner contradiction that guides the progress of the forms of Nature.*

'The Philosophy of Nature' is the philosophical and logical treatment of Nature. It presents Hegel's interpreta-

---

* Hegel holds that though Nature deals with the actually existing things such as matter, plants and animals, it is actually concerned with the thoughts of matter, plants and animals. While Logic deals with the thought of thought, Nature deals with the thought of things but not with Nature in its actuality. The thoughts of Logic are non-sensuous categories whereas the thoughts of Nature, as Hegel calls them, are non-sensuous notions.

tion of the physical and biological sciences of his time. It constitutes the application of formal concepts to natural phenomena. It is the illustration of the notions of thought that we find in Logic. It is a teleological way of viewing at 'things' that we find in Nature.

It is held by many a Hegelian that 'the Philosophy of Nature' deserves little attention because the scientific data that it contains are outmoded, because it suffers from the defect of external formalism of concepts that are arbitrarily applied to natural phenomena, and because it does not give a clear account of the relation between the notional framework of 'the Sciences of Logic' and the ever flourishing data of the positive science of Nature. 'The Philosophy of Nature' has earned a bad repute, since it is ridden with abstruse experimental illustrations and long citations from the scientific treatises of Hegel's time. As Findlay puts it, "This part of the system is one that many Hegelians have thought fit to ignore entirely."[2] Stace maintains that it is not only useless but also impossible to bring out the manifold deductions of the forms of Nature in detail. He says, "His (Hegel's) deductions in this sphere depend mostly upon far-fetched and fanciful analogies, and sometimes upon erroneous scientific information."[3]

However, since 'the Philosophy of Nature' forms an integral part of Hegel's system, it would be impertinent to ignore it altogether. A complete omission of it may result in a total misunderstanding of Hegel's system. The Logic and the Spirit would be left without any connection in the absence of Nature which performs the function of mediating them.

2. Findlay, J.N. Loc. cit., p. 267
3. Stace, Loc. cit., p. 315

This work, therefore, confines itself to a brief treatment of Hegel's dialectical development of Nature.*

Nature is divided into its main triad, viz., Mechanics, Physics and Organics. Mechanics is the study of inert matter that is impelled into action by external agency. Physics deals with matter which is in necessary and implicit relation with another matter. Organics comprises the study of Nature in its geological, botanical and zoological aspects. It is here that Nature passes from the inorganic to organic level.

Section A
MECHANICS

Let us now consider, in brief, the significant and salient determinations of Nature in Mechanics. Mechanics at first considers Nature in the simplest and vaguest form of its idea. It shows Nature as the blind and endless multiplicity of forms devoid of the principle of unity, viz., subjectivity or reason or notion. Later it relieves the abstract forms of Nature of their total indifference to each other by a unity which is merely ideal and not yet so realized as to give them an individuality. Mechanics exhibits itself in the triad, viz., space and time, the finite mechanics of matter and motion and the absolute mechanics of free motion.[4]

(i) *Space and Time*—Space is the most abstract notion with which the realm of Nature begins. Space is emptiness

4. Hegel, *Philosophy of Nature*, Op. cit., Vol. I, p. 221

* Hegel has devoted three volumes to cover the vast terrain of the Philosophy of Nature. But the noted Hegelians like Stace and Findlay who have dealt elaborately with Hegel's system as a whole, have devoted minimum space for the treatment of Nature. They have mainly shown the role of the Philosophy of Nature in Hegel's system.

devoid of any feature. It is an absolutely homogeneous continuity without any differentiation; it is a complete unity the content of which is different from itself; it is a non-sensuous sensibility in which the matter or sensuous things exist. Space is pure externality and abstraction in which all matter is contained. It corresponds to the category of being in Logic. Hegel writes, "The primary or immediate determination of Nature is the abstract universality of its self-externality, its unmediated indifference, i.e., space. It is on account of its being self-externality, that space constitutes collaterality of a completely ideal nature; as this extrinsicality is still completely abstract, space is simply continuous, and is devoid of any determinate difference."[5]

Hegel is of the view that the pure space implicitly exhibits the logical determinations of discreteness and continuity by breaking itself into 'heres' or points. That is, space in the form of points shows the "uneasy and struggling unity"[6] between discreteness and continuity. That is, space as points is both discrete and continuous, since points could both be separate ones and an unbroken process. The 'heres' or points could be juxtaposed without impinging one upon another. They do not constitute space. They are only a possibility of space. They are completely identical and therefore there is no true interruption or limit among them. So the discreteness or difference between the 'heres' is only abstract and completely implicit.

Apart from the 'heres', space manifests itself in its three dimensions, viz., length, breadth and depth. Hegel regards these dimensions as a reflection of the three notional determinations, viz., universality, specificity and individuality. But

5. Hegel, *Philosophy of Nature*, p. 223
6. Findlay, J. N., Loc. cit., p. 274

the difference between, these dimensions, like that of the 'heres' is not explicit. since space is only a form of mere quantity. The difference is only abstract but not definite. So it makes no difference whether we call the 'heres' continuous or discrete. So also, the spatial dimensions can be reduced to one of distance; it makes no difference whether we call a distance one of length or breadth or depth.[7]

Space passes on to time, since space can be regarded as points or as 'heres' only by the diremptive action of time. That is, the points or the 'heres' of space are comprehended through the movement of time, namely, the 'now'. The 'here' implies the 'now' and vice versa. Each is associated with the other. They are inseparable. Dialectically speaking time contains the truth of space. A point in space viz., 'here' is necessarily coupled with a moment of time, viz., 'now.' Thus space dialectically passes on to time. The passage is not subjective but strictly dialectical in the sense that space completes itself only by passing itself into time. Space negates itself in the form of time.[8]

Time has its own determinations; it determines itself in its three dimensions viz., past, present and future. But in time, only the 'present' is real. It is wrong to think of time as extended and as having the past, present and future as its real dimensions. For Hegel, time as 'present' or as eternity alone is real. He regards eternity but not duration as the notion of time. Eternity constitutes the absolute present moment of time whereas duration constitutes it as past, present and future. "Eternity will not be, nor has it been,

7. Findlay, J.N , Loc. cit., p. 275
8. Hegel, *Philosophy of Nature*, Op. cit., Vol. I, p. 229

it 'is'."[9] The notion of space and time passes to the finite mechanics of matter and motion, since space and time are 'constituted' by the matter only.

(ii) *The Finite Mechanics of Matter and Motion* : It is through things, namely matter, that we comprehend space and time. Space and time, devoid of matter, are purely abstract. Matter is the reality of space and time. The passage of space and time to matter can be put differently. As already mentioned, space and time manifest as 'here' and 'now.' The unity of 'here' and 'now' implies a place; and place necessarily implies a thing or matter; place without matter is inconceivable.[10]

Again, the notion of space and time not only passes to matter but also to motion, since motion is precisely the process of leaving behind the past 'heres' and 'nows' and reaching the future 'heres' and 'nows'. Motion is passing away and reinstatement of space and time. The notion of motion again, necessarily passes into the notion of matter, for motion of necessity implies 'something' which is movable. Motion without matter is inconceivable. Like space and time, matter and motion are inseparable. The one without the other is inconceivable. They are complementary to each other. Their reality is dialectical in the sense that each necessarily passes into the other.

Further, matter passes to gravity. Matter, of necessity, is the foundation of the two balancing forces, viz., repulsive force and attractive force. By offering resistance, matter repels itself from itself. It constitutes repulsion through which it posits its reality and fills space. As repulsion, matter

---

9. Hegel, *Philosophy of Nature*, Op. cit., p. 232,
10. Ibid., p. 236.

maintains a difference within itself by holding itself apart from itself. As attraction, matter exhibits the complete sameness of what held apart by repulsion. Gravity, according to Hegel, is the togetherness of two forces of matter. It is the perpetual acknowledgement of the real nullity of the mutual outsideness of matter. So gravity is the unifying principle of matter. It is the notional or the rational principle of matter.[11]

Gravity manifests itself in its triadic form, viz., inertia, impact and fall. Inertia is matter which is inert. Matter not only gravitates but exhibits inertia. Inertia constitutes the sublated reality of matter. Hegel is of the view that inertia is necessarily related to gravity, since every material body depends on a balance between the diremptive tendencies of inertia and the unifying tendencies of gravitation. Matter is not only inert but receives or imparts motion through the impact with other bodies. Impact not only generates motion but also resists it. Impact which generates motion in matter passes to the notion of fall, for motion determines itself in two ways, viz., (1) direction, and (2) fall. That is, motion manifests itself as a fall to a certain direction. Fall is essential motion which is affected when bodies are separated from their centre of gravity by relatively empty space.

Fall, according to Hegel, is relatively free motion; it is free in the sense that it is posited through the action of the body; it is the manifestation of body's own gravity. At the same time, fall is conditioned since it is the primary negation of externality. Fall as separation from the connection with the centre is contingent.[12] So the notion of fall is not completely free. It is not absolutely free but conditioned as well

11. Hegel, *Philosophy of Nature*, Op. cit., pp. 242-3
12. Ibid., pp. 253-4

as free. So the notion of fall passes to absolute mechanics where matter is completely free.

(iii) *Absolute Mechanics*: Hegel takes the solar system as an example of absolute mechanics wherein gravitation working in triadic notional determinations—universal, particular and individual—is found. Hegel regards the Sun as the universal centre (which is immobile and around which all matter necessarily organizes itself), the planets as particular centres and the satellites and comets as individual elements. Here gravitation as the unitary principle, governs allm atter in Nature. Hegel equates gravitation in solar system with the principle of thought which is the unitary principle of the universe. This shows that nothing in the universe is accidental but a necessary organization of matter round the Sun, the planets, the satellites and the many subordinate centres which move in circles.[13]

Thus, in Mechanics, Hegel uses the dialectic to make 'explicit' the implicit interconnections between the various forms of matter. As Findlay puts it "The dialectical method here plainly appears as the simple undoing of initial abstractions."[14]

In Mechanics, matter is considered in its abstraction and quantity. But matter has yet to be conceived in its particularity or specificity of reflection and of having qualities of its own. Therefore, Mechanics passes on to physics wherein matter is studied in its essential relativity and reflectedness.

13. Hegel, *Philosophy of Nature* Op. cit., pp. 260-61
14. Findlay, J. N., Loc. cit., p. 276

Section B

PHYSICS

The realm of physics comprises three kinds of sub-notions, viz., (i) physics of universal individuality, (ii) physics of specific individuality and (iii) physics of total individuality.

(i) *The Physics of Universal Individuatity* : The physics of universal individuality deals with the various physical elements namely, light, air, fire, water and earth, out of which the natural world is constituted. Hegel conceives light as the medium or agent which holds the material world together. It is the being of absolute velocity; it is the pure materiality, the actual existence of which lies within itself. It is actuality which as a transparent possibility brings everything into universal connection. In Hegel's words, "Matter in its primary qualified state is pure self-identity, unity of intro-reflection; as such it is the primary manifestation and is itself still abstract. As existent in nature, it is independent, self-relation opposed to the other determinations of totality. This existing and universal self of matter is light, which as individuality is the star, and as moment of totality, the Sun."[15]

Hegel passes on from light to the other four elements of nature, viz., air, fire, water and earth. Air is an element of negative universality. Unlike light it is heavy. It is through air that everything is revealed to everything in the slowly diffused and quasimaterial form of fragrance. Hegel says, "It is in fact air, a fluidity which is transparent and passive with regard to light, but which sublimates all individuality within itself and which by its mechanical elasticity, pervades everything."[16] The element of air passes to the elements of

15. Hegel, *Philosophy af Nature*, Op. cit., Vol. II, p. 11
16. Ibid., p. 36

opposition, viz., fire and water. Fire is the opposite of air. The character of fire is to consume and destroy. It eats up what is the other. It resembles the tooth of time and the self-assertive universality of the ego. In Hegel's words "In itself air is fire, and it shows this when it is compressed. It is posited in fire as negative universality or self-relating negativity. Fire is materialized time, or self-hood in which light is identical with heat."[17]

The next element in the notion of the elements of opposition is water. Water is an element of passive neutrality and a universal solvent which adheres to all things and wets them. In water fiery processes quench themselves; in itself water is without cohesion, smell, taste, form or opacity.[18] Water is the element of selfless opposition or being-for-other. It is the abstract neutrality but not individualized neutrality like salt. From very early times water is called the mother of everything particular. The notion of water proceeds to the notion of earth. Earth is the notion of individual determinateness and developed difference. It represents the hard and definite aspects of nature. The notion of earth passes to the notion of meteorology.

Meteorology is determined by the transmutation of the elements into one another. This transmutation is quite unknown to finite physics, in which the understanding always holds fast to the persistence of abstract identity, whereby the elements, being composite, are merely dispersed and separated, but not really transmuted. Water, air, fire and earth are in conflict within this elementary process. Water is the existent material of the process. Air is the unobstrusive, destructive principle. It posits that which is of an ideal nature. It is the

---

17. Hegel, *Philosophy of Nature*, Op. cit., p. 58
18. Ibid., pp. 39-40

activity which sublates determinate being. Fire is the appearance of being-for-self. It is ideality which attains the moment of appearance in which destruction becomes evident. Therefore the simplicity of the relationship is that water is transformed into air and conversely, air becomes water, and breaks out of being-for-self into the inert neutrality of its opposite, which for its part tends to become being-for-self. Hegel says, "The individual identity which binds the different elements, as well as the variety which they exhibit both amongst themselves and with regard to their unity, is a dialectic which constitutes the physical life of the earth, the meteorological process. It is in this process alone that the elements, as dependent moments, have their subsistence, their existence being generated and posited within it, after having been developed out of implicitness as moments of the Notion."[19]

Thought in Mechanics is not adequate. In it, we had merely the several determinations of weighted matter or gravity. In physics, thought progresses a little further. Here matter exhibits its real nature in self-hood. Self-determined nature of light, which is the opposite of weighted matter, is the matter's self-hood. In Physics, instead of one general individuality, we have a multiplication of individualites. Each individuality has the form of the whole within it. Now the physics of universal individuality passes to the physics of particular or specific individuality.

(ii) *Physics of Particular or Specific Individuality* : In the physics of particular or specific individuality, Hegel deals with four material properties, viz., specific gravity, cohesion, sound and warmth. Under these notions Hegel deals with an ascending series of determinations in which matter become more and

19. Hegel, *Philosophy of Nature*, Op. cit., p. 42

more self-centred and bestows a unifying and distinctive individuality on all its parts.

Gravity and space are not separated in the determinateness. The distinction between bodies is only one of mass which is merely a difference of one body from another. The difference is measured by the amount of space filled. A different measure takes place in being-in self, where different weights occupy equal space and the equal weights occupy different spaces. This inherent relationship of space and gravity forms the self-hood of specific gravity of a material thing. This spacific gravity is being-in and far-self, which relates itself only to itself and completely indifferent to mass. For instance, the volume of a cubic inch of water is equal to a cubic inch of gold; but their weights are entirely different. Gold is nineteen times heavier than water. And also a pound of water occupies nineteen times more space than a pound of gold. Here the pure quantitativeness gives way to qualitativeness. Now matter has its own determination within itself. Specific gravity, being the fundamental determination of matter pervades bodies. In Hegel's words, "The simple abstract specification of matter is its specific gravity or density. In this, the weight of the mass is related to the volume and it is by means of this that material self-hood tears itself away, from the universal gravity of its abstract relationship to the central body, ceases to be the uniform content of space, and opposes abstract extrinsicality with a specific being-in-self."[20]

Now thought proceeds to cohesion. Cohesion is a determinateness which differentiates itself from gravity. It is not only a general centrality, but also a centre related to a plurality of parts. It is a comparison of bodies according to

20. Ibid., p. 57.

specific gravity. It is not the totality of the determination; it is still a moment of determination opposed to gravity. Cohesion passes to adhesion. Adhesion is affinity with something more than self but not being-in-self. For instance, light in its neutrality is adhesive. Light is when it shines or shows itself in something else. Water is also adhesive in its neutrality. It makes things wet. Adhesive passes to coherence. It is the ratio of the intensity of the coherence to the weight of the body. Hence if a part or a mass is pulled or pressed by weight it counteracts with a certain quantity of its being-in-self.[21] This is called quantitative coherence which passes to qualitative coherence. The qualitative coherence consists of homogeneous masses with an inherent characteristic form. It becomes explicit as the abstract dimensions of space. The qualitative coherence passes to the elasticity.

When cohesion displays itself in motion then elasticity comes on the scene. Elasticity is nothing but the cohesion itself in motion. Hegel says that cohesion and coherence are abstract elasticity directed outward. Now it passes to the elasticity which is internal to the self individualising body. Elasticity is the movement of the body, by which it repels itself from itself. It is being-for self. Elasticity passes to the next notion, namely, sound which is being-for-other.

Sound is associated with weighted matter. It belongs to the mechanical sphere. Though sound is attached to the mechanical sphere, it is a free and physical expression of ideal nature. Sound is free from weighted matter but it is of matter simultaneously. For instance, bodies or forms resound only when they are struck, but they do not sound of their own accord as organic bodies do. Sound by itself is the self of individuality which includes matter and form. Sound passes

21. Ibid., p. 64.

to the heat or warmth. Sound and heat are directly related to each other. Heat is the consummation of sound and distinguishes itself as the negativity of this material being. Heat is the negation of sound. So it is the negation of negation. Hegel says, "The sonorous bodies will grow hot when they are struck or rubbed together, and it is in this phenomenon that heat originates with sound in conformity with the Notion."[22]

(iii) *Physics of Total Individuality* : Now Hegel passes from the physics of particular individuality to the physics of total individuality which contains innumerable subdivisions within itself. It is not necessary to go into the details of their content. Neither is it possible to give a full treatment of these notions. Let us now simply enumerate the various notion of the physics of total individuality which is divided into (1) the phenomena of shape, (2) the properties of bodies and (3) the chemical process. The phenomena of shape is divided into a triad viz., shapelessness, magnetism and crystal. The properties of bodies is divided into the triad, viz., the relationship of individual body, the properties of opposition and electricity. The relationship of individual body to light, is again divided into its three sub-notions, viz., transparency, refraction and the theory of colors. The notion of chemical process is divided into its triad viz., synsomation, the real chemical process and the process of separation which have their sub-triads.

Here the important point of observation is that in the physics of total individuality, Hegel pictures the chemical process as exhibiting animation which is the origin of life. He holds that the real chemical process is not material process

22. Ibid., p. 81.

but a vital process which contains notion of Reason as its unifying principle. The vital process is a concrete unity assembling itself out of distinct parts and functions. The vital process which is both being-in-itself and being-for-self represents the presence of an organic notion, namely, the principle of Reason. Thus Hegel passes from Physics to Organics.[23]

Section C

ORGANICS

The notion of Organics is the guiding star in the whole course of dialectical evolution, since it is in Organics that the Idea comes to existence or life and attains the highest level of Nature in the form of self-conscious spirit which refers itself to itself. Organics is the synthesis of Mechanics, the thesis and Physics, the antithesis. To put it in terms of ideal determinations, Organics is individuality while Mechanics is universality and Physics is particularity. The notion of Organics is divided into its triad, viz., the geological organism, the vegetable organism and the animal organism.

(i) *Geological Organism*—The notion of geological organism deals mainly with the nature of the planet earth. Hegel regards earth as a huge corpse which is an embodiment of living beings. Earth is a totality whereas all its corporealities are particularities. It is a seat of an indefinite number of spontaneously generated living beings. The geological organism is divided into its triad, viz., the history of earth, structural composition and the life of the earth. The notion of the history of the earth is again divided into its sub-triad, viz., the powers of the terrestrial process, geognosy and the physical geography. In all these triads and sub-triads, Hegel

23. Findlay, J. N., Loc. cit., p. 283.

studies the formation of the planet earth and its various processes viz., terrestial, magnetic, chemical, electrical, meteorology. He studies the formation of land, atmosphere, water, islands, valleys, rocks, and continents of the earth. Under the notion of physical geography, Hegel maintains that the formation of the earth may appear to the sensuous consciousness as accidental and contingent. But Reason can comprehend the truth that there is the determination of notion in the formation of the earth's geography. He maintains that there is the activity of notion even behind the formation of continents. The continental formation is not contingent but rational. Germany is formed as the centre of Europe.[24] However, the dialectical structure of the notion of geological organism is outdated; its dialectical transitions from one notion to the other are obscure; the links between the sub-notions of the geological organism are flimsy. The illustrations of the geological organism do not match the notions of Reason exactly. Therefore, this part of the system, as Findlay puts it hardly deserves a detailed study and comment.[25]

The geological organism passes on to the vegetable organism which deals with plant life wherein there is the beginning of the subjective life without being objective to itself. Hegel makes a transition from the geological to the vegetable through the notions of the forms of life that are intermediary in the sense of being both inorganic and organic. He takes mildew, fungi rnd lichens as inter-mediary forms of life. It is difficult to classify these life-forms with certainty. Hegel treats these transitory forms of life as providing a good means of dialectical transition to the vegetable organism.[26]

---

24. Hegel, *Philosophy of Nature*, Op. cit., Vol. III, p. 24.
25. Findlay, J. N., Loc. cit., p. 284.
26. Ibid.

(ii) *Vegetable Organism*—Hegel holds that in vegetable organism, thought progresses from the objective realm to the realm of subjectivity. But the unity of the subject and object in the vegetable organism is yet immediate and implicit but not distinct. Hegel says, "In plant which is merely subjective animation in its primary immediacy, the objective organism and its subjectivity are still immediately identical."[27] The notion of vegetable organism gets divided into its main triad viz., the morphological process, the process of assimilation and the process of reproduction.

In the notion of morphological process, Hegel studies extensively about the process of the formation of the germ, the wood-formation and the bud-formation in plant life. It includes the study of the process of the formation of the root, the leaf, the cells, the tissues and the vessels. It studies about the activity of the saps that leads to the formation of the wood. It also studies about the processes of the formation of the buds, flowers, fruits and seeds in plant life. Hegel discusses it in greater detail in the notion of reproduction. Here Hegel tries to unfold the entire structure of the notion of the plant.[28]

The morphological process, through the formation of the bud, passes on to the notion of the process of assimilation. The morphological process deals mainly with the internal structure of the plant whereas the process of assimilation deals with the external life of the necessary elements, namely, light, earth, water and air without which the plant life would be impossible. The seed becomes the plant and the plant again produces the seed only because of the necessary relation of

---

27. Hegel, *Philosophy of Nature*, Op. cit., Vol. III, p. 45.
28. Ibid., pp. 80-82.

the plant to the earth, water, light and air. Hegel says, "The seed only germinates when it is stimulated from without. What is more, the diremption of the plant-form into root and leaf is itself a diremption directed towards the earth and water, and towards the light and air."[29] The plant can be upright and its various aspects acquire their vigour only through the element of light. The plant consolidates its own individuality only through the absolute of power of light. Air is necessary since the plant life includes the process of respiration. The plant inhales carbondioxide and exhales oxygen. So also water is necessary for the seed to become a plant. Devoid of water, the seed or germ remain for years without any vital impulse or germination. The process of assimilation proceeds to the process of reproduction which is the generic process of the vegetable organism. In the process of reproduction the plant preserves itself by constantly producing the other individuals of its own kind. Hegel regards it as the moment of the plant's actualisation which it exhibits upon itself.

Hegel treats the process of fertilisation or reproduction in plant life as the internal resumption of individuality of the plant. In reproduction the bud disappears as soon as it blossoms into the flower which gradually modifies itself into fruit, which in turn gives seeds for a new plant. Thus in the notion of reproduction, the plant preserves itself by producing another plant. Here, Hegel pictures the vegetable organism as bringing about its organic nature from itself and by means of itself. The process of reproduction which is the generic process of the vegetable organism proceeds to the notion of animal organism.

---

29. Ibid., pp. 83-84.

(iii) *Animal Organism*—Animal organism is the synthesis of geological and plant organism. As we have seen already, plant organism mediates or acts as a link between the two. Hegel treats animal organism as a true organism "whose form agrees with its notion, which has parts that are truly members, and a "subjectivity" which exists as the pervasive unity of the whole."[30] Animal organism has subjectivity which can be object to itself. Therefore animal organism is being-for-itself and an existent unity of differences. In animal organism, form agrees with its notion; it has parts which are truly members; it has a subjectivity which exitts as the pervasive unity of the whole. It is an organic whole of the many parts. In it, organic individuality exists as subjectivity; it preserves within itself the unity of self-hood. The self-hood "constitutes the nature of the animal, in which the actuality and externality of immediate singularity is countered by the introreflected self of singularity or the subjective universality which is within itself."[31]

In animal organism, Hegel regards voice as one of its distinctive characters. Inorganic objects produce sound only when they are struck while animals produce sounds spontaneously. Each animal has a distinct voice.[32]

From these general characteristics, Hegel passes on to the fundamental characteristics of animal organism, viz., sensibility, irritability and reproduction. Sensibility is the presence of spirit in the form of ego in the organism. It is the testimony of the presence of subjectivity in the organism. Sensibility passes into irritability when an organism is touched

30. Findlay, J. N., Loc. cit., p. 286.
31. Hegel, *Philosophy of Nature,* Op. cit., Vol. III, p. 102.
32. Findlay, J. N., Loc. cit., p. 286.

by another organism. Irritability is stimulation by another; it is the reaction of the organism (against the other) for self-preservation.[33] Reproduction is the infinite negativity which produces another out of the organism. It constitutes the actuality of the animal organism. It passes through sensibility and irritability and absorbs them. The notions of sensibility, irritability and reproduction are related to the nervous, the muscular and the vascular and to the digestive and glandular systems respectively. Here, Hegel deals extensively with the entire physiology of the animal organism which includes the functions, the structures of the sense organs and the animal drives and instincts, the detailed treatment of which is tedious and unnecessary.

With this general and fundamental characteristics, Hegel divides the notion of animal organism into its main triad viz., the notoin of shape, the notion of assimilation and the notion of generic process. In the notion of shape Hegel speaks of the formation of bone which gives shape to the animal organism. Bone is one of the distinctive characters of animal organism. It is on the basis of the bone that the animal first establishes itself as animal. Just as wood in plants, bone belongs to the shape of the animal organism. Hegel treats bone as the immediately sensible moment of shape. Bone as skeleton, gives the organism its primary determination as something stable and hard. Bone extends itself into firm determinations such as horns and claws. Hegel treats the spinal column as the basis of all animal shapes. He treats it as the main bone and all other bones as its modifications.[34] The notion of shape has its own sub-notions which need not be

33. Hegel, *Philosophy of Nature,* Op. cit., Vol. III, p. **112**.
34. Ibid., p. 114.

dealt with in detail. On the whole, in the notion of shape, Hegel studies the inner nature of the animal organism. The notion of shape proceeds to the notion of the process of assimilation which deals with the outwardness of the animal organism.[35] It is divided into its sub-notions viz., (1) theoretical process, (2) practical process and (3) the nisus formatives. In the theoretical process of assimilation, Hegel deals with sensations like sight, smell, etc. and with their related factors like the sense of colour, odour etc.[36] In the notion of the practical process of assimilation, Hegel deals with the internal diremption of self which manifests itself in appetite and will in the animal organism. It includes the study of the process of thirst, the breathing process, the cutaneous process and the digestive process and the process of excretion. Here Hegel deals with the functioning of the alimental and intestinal canals, the secretion of the juices like bile, gastric and pancreatic.[37]

The process of assimilation through its final category of excretion proceeds to the notion of nisus formation. The nisus formation is the unity of theoretical and practical processes of assimilation. The product of assimilation is inorganic matter which is external to the animal; it remains external even after assimilation. Hence the nisus formatives resemble excretion by self-externalising itself. It reproduces the form of the organism within the external world. The object is formed in a way that the subjective need is satisfied. For example, appetite is satisfied and restrained simultaneously. The organism only objectifies itself by disposing of inorganic material for its own purpose. In the nisus formatives, the organism

35. Ibid., p. 137.
36. Ibid., pp. 139-40.
37. Ibid., pp. 148-49 & 162.

attains to the self-enjoyment of determinate sentience.[38] The nisus formation which is relative totality of the theoretic and practical processes of assimilation proceeds to the generic process of animal organism.

The generic process of organism deals with the sexual relationship, the genus and the species and the genus and the individual. The notion of sexual relationship deals with the formation and function of the genital organs in the male and female sexes.[39] In the notion of the genus and species and the genus the individual, Hegel classifies the animal kingdom by determining the universal character of a certain kind of animals. The classification takes certain features, habits and blood of the species as the basis. Hegel classifies the animal kingdom into three groups : (1) worms, mollusca and shell-fish etc., (2) insects and (3) vertebrate. The vertebrate is classified into its sub-classes, viz., (1) fish (2) amphibia (3) birds and (4) mammals. Mammals are treated as the higher form of animals, since they exhibit all the organs in their fully formed state. The distinctive character of the mammals is to feed their young from their bodies. Hegel regards them as the most unselfish of all animals.[40] Hegel classifies mammals into four group basing on their teeth, feet, claws etc., viz., (1) animals with hands, (2) animals with claws, (3) animals with hoofs and (4) animals with fins. The notion of mammals passes on the notion of medical science which is divided into its triad, viz., (1) the disease of the individual (2) healing therapy and (3) the death of the individual of its own accord. Hegel is of the view that the individual contacts disease by entering into contact with certain specific noxious influences

38. Ibid., p. 166.
39. Ibid., p. 175.
40. Ibid., p. 188.

from without. The state of disease is a disproportion between the organic self and its determinate being. Hegel divides disease into three kinds : (1) the acute (2) the chronic and (3) the disease of the soul. Acute diseases have their seat in the organism as a whole. The chronic disease is that which does not spread to the whole of the organism. It confines to a single part of the organism. It is difficult to cure chronic diseases. The disease of the soul is caused by terror and grief which may lead the organism to death.[41] The notion of disease passes on to the notion of healing therapy which is of three kinds, viz., (1) positive stimulus, (2) negative stimulus and (3) mesmerism. According to Hegel therapy is the antithesis of disease. In disease the organism is under the power of something other than itself while in therapy the organism is released from the power of an alien organism. In therapy, the organism resumes its normal state and comes under its own power. The positive stimulus of therapy stimulates the orgahism to digest the negative element in it. It restores the organism to the general activity of assimilation. Hegel treats the easily digestible food as the medicine of positive stimulus. The negative stimulus is treating the disease by suspending all the activity of the organism. In it, the inner vitality of organism is encouraged by eliminating the external and objective treatment. Hegel regards homeopathy and fasting as the examples of the negative stimulus. Mesmerism is the treatment of the disease of the soul. It relieves the organism of its grief and terror and puts it to sleep.[42] Mesmerism proceeds to the death of the individual of its own accord. Hegel holds that death is the very nature of the organism. Death lies in the very heart of the organism. Disease is only

41. Ibid., pp. 194-98.
42. Ibid., pp. 205-08.

the external cause of death and is not the real ground of death. Disease may be cured, but death is the necessity of the organism. Therefore death occurs in the form of old age which manifests in the lack of strength, the slackening of muscles and tendons, bad digestion and feeble sensation. Death is a retreat of the organism from the individual to the purely vegetative life. Through death, the organism, according to Hegel, attains the universal. Thus in Nature, the universality makes its appearance in its negative way by sublating the subjectivity. Hegel says that it is from the dead material of the Nature that the Spirit arises. The aim of the dialectical development of Nature is to meet its own death by breaking through the rind of its sensory externality. It is to burn itself like phoenix and rejuvenate itself as Spirit, which is the universality of conscious thought. Thus, the notion which exists in Nature as being-in-itself, has now become being-for-self.[43]

---

43. Ibid., pp. 210-12.

CHAPTER IV

DIALECTIC IN HEGEL'S PHILOSOPHY OF SPIRIT

Introduction

In chapter II, 'Dialectic in Hegel's Science of Logic', we have dealt with the dialectical evolution of the Idea or Reason as being confined to the realm of pure thought. Here, the Idea is comprehended in its immediacy and as being-in-self. In chapter III, 'Dialectic in Hegel's Philosophy of Nature,' we have seen the dialectical movement of Reason as externalizing itself in the form of nature. In Hegel's 'Philosophy of Nature' the Idea is comprehended in its mediacy and as being-for-self. In the present chapter, 'Dialectic in Hegel's Philosophy of Spirit', we propose to deal with the dialectical movement of the Idea as returning to itself from the externality of Nature. Here, the Idea is comprehended as the unity of immediacy and mediacy, and being-in and for self. In the realm of Spirit, the Idea manifests itself as the living and concrete being of man actually existing in the world. As Hegel describes it, Spirit is the self-knowing actual Idea raised to the concept of the living spirit which is necessarily wise and draws distinctions in itself and returns to unity with itself out of its distinctions.[1]

The realm of Spirit is divided into its main triad, viz., the Subjective Spirit, the Objective and the Absolute Spirit.

---

1. Hegel, *Phenomenology of Mind*, Translated by J.B. Baillie, George Allen & Unwin Ltd., London, Second edition, 1949, Translators Introductions, pp. 31-32.

Section A
THE SUBJECTIVE SPIRIT

The Subjective Spirit is divided into its triad viz., anthropology, phenomenology and psychology on the basis of the level of consciousness manifested by the Spirit. In anthropology the Spirit is in a state of sleep or semi-conscious. In phenomenology it is conscious and in psychology it is self-conscious.

(i) *Anthropology*

Anthropology is the study of the Idea which has 'emerged' from Nature as soul. The Idea as soul* is the lowest conceivable phase of Spirit. It is termed as Spirit in sleep, a vague semi-consciousness that can realize nothing; it is still in the grip of Nature and hardly above the level of animality.

Anthropology is divided into its triad, viz., the natural soul, the feeling soul and the actual soul. The natural soul in its immediacy is in bondage to Nature; it is a sort of psychic life diffused throughout the Nature and not yet divided into separate individual souls. The natural soul is again divided into its triad, viz., physical qualities, physical alterations and sensibility. The physical qualities of the natural soul are determined by the environment out of which it emerges. The natural soul is what the environment makes it to be. Its

---

* We have to distinguish Hegel's conception of 'soul' from what is usually referred to as 'soul' (Atman) in Indian Philosophical tradition. In the orthodox schools of Indian Philosophy 'soul' stands for the principle of consciousness or the seat of consciousness as opposed to body (matter). 'Soul', for Hegel, stands for the lowest conceivable phase of the Spirit in the course of its evolution.

physical qualities are affected by the planetary system also. The physical alterations stand for changes that the natural soul undergoes. They are of two types, viz , essential and accidental. The essential alterations are the changes in childhood, youth, manhood and oldage.* The accidental alterations are the changes in sexual relations and those we experience in sleeping and waking states. Sensibility refers to the sensation of physical qualities by the soul. The physical qualities or the sensations are different from the soul. The soul possesses them as something different from itself.[2] But the distinction between them is internal. The sensations are not objective but purely subjective** like hunger, pain, fatigue, etc.

The feeling soul is that which is aware of its sensations. "It is the soul which feels and the soul so viewed is the feeling soul."[3] It is of three kinds viz , feeling soul in its immediacy, self-feeling and habit. The feeling soul in its immediacy is that which is aware of 'self' or 'I' with a feeling of difference between itself and another 'self' or 'I' upon which it is acting. Hegel takes the child in its mother's womb and hypnosis as the examples of the feeling soul in its immediacy, wherein the soul of the child or that of a person under hypnosis is governed and controlled by the mother or the hypnotist. The

---

* The natural soul and its deduction may be logically perfect but the detailed physical qualities and examples given seem to be arbitrarily deduced and empirically picked up.

** There is difference between sensibility and sensuous consciousness. For Hegel sensuous consciousness means the consciousness which senses give about external objects.

2. Stace, W.T., Loc. cit., p. 332.
3. Ibid., p. 334.

The soul of self-feeling is that which is aware of itself without the aid of the other. For example, I am aware of myself. Habit stands for the continual repetition of particular sensations and feelings by the soul.

(ii) *Phenomenology*

When we pass from anthropology to phenomenology we pass from soul to consciousness. In anthropology the relation of soul to its content* was implicit and abstract whereas in phenomenology it becomes explicit and concrete. Whereas in anthropology soul and its content remain indistinct, in phenomenology it becomes distinct. In other words, in phenomenology consciousness is comprehended as something over and above its content. Here the soul and its content are treated as opposites. Hegel calls the soul which is distinct from its content consciousness. Phenomenology is the study of such consciousness in its three stages, viz., consciousness proper, self-consciousness and reason. Consciousness proper at this stage is that which the object is independent of consciousness proper which Hegel terms as subject. It has three stages to pass through viz., sensuous-consciousness or sense-certainty, sense-preception and intellect or understanding. To Hegel sensuous-consciousness is that wherein the relation subject and object is immediate. It makes an object 'this' or 'that'. In it, the object is directly presented to consciousness as being 'there'. It is known in certainty without any mediating link. Sense-certainty knows that the object 'is'. I knows the object as nothing else, but a mere 'otherness' which is abstract. It is crude sensation of object without shape or form.[4] Hegel holds that the state of mind as sense-certainty

* Sensation and feeling constitute the content of the soul.

4. Hegel, *Phenomenology of Mind*, Op. cit., pp. 149ff.

does not belong to human being but to lower species only. Sense-perception, the next stage of consciousness proper refers to the understanding of the universal in relation to another universal. Here, a universality is introduced by the spontaneous activity of the mind only.[5] In it, the universality is only sensuous. It deals with the sensuous universals like table, house, river, star, animal, etc. And in intellect the third stage, the mind passes to non-sensuous universal like force, gravitation, law, many, one, etc. which are pure, real and non-perceptible. Intellect conceives behind the sensuous world of a multiplicity of supersensuous world of universals which manifest themselves in the multiplicity of the sensuous world.[6] Hegel regards the supersensuous as reality and the sensuous as appearance. The former is self-subsistent and the latter depends upon the former. It constitutes the universal law upon which the latter is founded. The business of intellect is to find the true reality of all particular things by explaining and referring them their laws. Intellect proceeds to the category of self-consciousness.

Self-consciouness is the stage in which the subject sees itself in the object like a person sees his own image or reflection in mirror. Here, there is yet the division and contradiction between the consciousness proper, the 'I' and its object, the 'not-I'. The development of self-consciousness passes through three stages. They are (1) appetite or desire; (2) self-consciousness recognitive; and (3) universal self-consciousness. Appetite or desire is the ending of division between the subject and the object. It is the 'impulse' to abolish the independence of the object. It expresses itself by destroying or consuming

---

5. Ibid., pp. 162ff.
6. Ibid., pp. 177-78.

the object. Hegel gives 'hunger' as an example of desire.[7] Desire passes to self-consciousness recognitive wherein the mind recognizes the existence of other selves. Here the object of the mind is another self similar to it.* It is the recognition by the ego of the existence of other egos in the world. The egos in the world are so interconnected that one cannot destroy the other. For instance, the master cannot afford to kill the slave, since the death of the slave implies the ending of his lordship over the slave. The master desires only to reduce the slave to a slave 'thing'.[8] The master realises his independence by acting upon the slave. And the slave recognizes his independence in the act of moulding the object he works upon. Here, it is not only the master who recognizes himself as self-conscious but recognizes the slave also as self-conscious. So also, the slave recognizes as independent not only himself but also his object, for it is the independence of the object which constitutes consciousness proper, and the abolition of this independence brings about the development of self-consciousness.[9] Thus, the universal self-consciousness is the mutual recognition of all egos by each other as being equally self-conscious. The universal self-consciousness passes to the category of reason.

---

* Here the transition from 'thing' to 'self' seems to be very obscure. The transition from the object of desire to another self appears to be fantastic, but it will be meaningful when we regard transition as only a logical. For Hegel, transition from one category to the other is not one of time but logic. The idea of another self is implicit in the object of desire and can be logically deduced from it.

7. Ibid., p. 225.
8. Ibid., pp. 234-35.
9. Stace, W.T., Loc. cit., p. 359.

Reason, the last stage of the realm of phenomenology, is the synthesis of consciousness proper and self-consciousness. It is the principle of the identity of opposites. Here subject and object are comprehended as being identical and different at the same time. The subject and object pass into each other. The object is no more totally independent and distinct from the subject or consciousness which Hegel calls reason. Reason recognizes everything other than itself as being there to enrich itself as self-consciousness. This is precisely the meaning of Hegel's Idealism of Reason. As Findlay says, "The Idealism of Reason means that objects are all in a deep sense mine-mine to understand, mine to experiment with, mine to remould and mine to find myself in—and that the categories of Reason, its varying a priori concepts of objects, are no more than the ways in which such objects can be made mine, in which they can make an enriching contribution to my self-consciousness."[10] Now the dialectic passes on to the realm of psychology, wherein reason as mind is comprehended in its various manifestations.

(iii) *Psychology*

In psychology, the mind* is shown as the highest moment of reason. Here, the mind is the Subjective Spirit in

---

* The term "Geist" is translated as Spirit of Mind is used to describe the subject matter of the *Philosophy of Spirit* in general. It has two meanings for Hegel viz., (1) It signifies in general, the spiritual being which begins in anthropology and continues throughout the whole philosophy of Spirit; (2) it signifies in particular, the highest phase of Subjective Spirit which constitutes the subject matter of psychology.

10. Findlay, J.N., Loc. cit., p. 103.

and for-itself. In it, the Spirit sees its object as no more an alien and independent reality. Instead, it recognizes the object as itself and comprehends itself to be all reality. The mind, in psychology passes through three phases, viz., (1) theoretical mind i.e., cognition, (2) the practical mind i.e., volition and (3) free mind.

Theoretical mind is that in which the seemingly strange object looses its character of the merely given and gets absorbed into the rational life of the subject. This is explained clearly in three stages viz., (1) direct intuitive acquaintance (2) imaginative reproduction and (3) pure thinking.

In direct intuitive* acquintance sensation is capable of containing a highly intellectual content in a nutshell. It is the immediacy of mind which is free. Although it has the nature of judgment, it is not a judgment proper, because it involves no mediation. It is the instinctive perception of a fact which any one can experience without assigning any reason. "Intuition is a consciousness filled with the certitude of reason, whose object has the character of being reasonable. not accordingly an individual torn apart into distinct sides but a totality, a coherent fulness of determinations......."[11]

Intuition involves two factors viz., attention and feeling. Attention is the pure inner feeling of the direction of the mind It is a free mind in which, the ego collects itself together and concentrates itself in a special way. Feeling involves a reference to objectivity. It is not purely a subjective act but an outwardization of the inward feeling as smoothing existent.

---

* Direct intuitive acquaintance is different from sensation or the sense awareness as we have seen in anthropology and also in phenomenology.

11. Ibid., pp. 302-03.

Hegel regards intuition as fully developed when attention and outwardization are present in it. Intuition passes to the next category called imaginative reproduction which goes through three stages, viz., (1) recollection, (2) imagination and (3) memory. Recollection is recalling whenever necessary—what is stored up in the sub-conscious. It is otherwise called remembrance. It passes to the category of imagination which is the (result of) continuous production of images from thc sub-conscious. It is a flow of images which are representative or universal in character. Each image stands for something more than itself which is universal. For instance, the particular image of the lion becomes the sign of lions in general. The concept of imagination passes to the category of memory. Memory is thinking in names which stand for the universal and do the work of recollection by a flow of imagery. Hegel says that we think in names. When the name is given we need neither the actual vision nor the image of the animal. The name is the unimaged simple representation.[12]

The category of memory passes to the category of thought or thinking. Hegel says that thought arises when the image as an image is suppressed. Thinking is the understanding of the name without images. The very fact that thought is usually accompanied by imagery implies that thought by itself is without images. Thought is a unity of universality and being or subjectivity and objectivity. It overlaps the distinction between itself and being. Hegel says, "It knows that what thought is, and that what is, only is in so far as it is a thought."[13] The category of thought proceeds dialectically to the higher category viz., practical mind or will which

12. Stace, W. T., Loc. cit., p. 366.
13. Ibid., p. 367.

acts upon the world. The activity of will moulds its object. It has three sub-categories namely, practical feeling, impulses and choice, and happiness.

Practical feeling is an instinct of the will which immediately finds its content or the world either conformable or not conformable to itself. The very nature of the practical feeling is that it cannot leave its content, the world as it is. The very essence of it to act upon and shape its content. And the impulse is propensity of the will to act on the content. Impulse becomes passion when thought as practical feeling throws itself wholly into the fulfilment of a single impulse to the exclusion of all others. Impulse is multiple and will is one. The former is particular and latter is universal and always distinguishes itself the diversity of impulses. It stands above and chooses between them. The category of impulses and choice proceeds to the category of happiness.

Thought as will does not get completely satisfied in the gratification of the impulses since a particular impulse with its particular object can give only a particular satisfaction. Since the will is universal, it seeks to attain a universal satisfaction which is possible only by making its content universal and conform to itself. The universal satisfaction which the will seeks is called happiness. The category of happiness passes to the category of free mind since the will fails to attain universal satisfaction even in happiness. The universal satisfaction which the will seeks in happiness can only be pursued through and by means of the particular impulses. Since the will can never find true satisfaction through impulses, it has to find a remedy to its dissatisfaction by making itself its own object by putting itself forth into the world. And the process through which the will makes itself its object is called free mind. Free mind is will which has itself for its object. It is otherwise called free will, which is not limited by another. Unlike in impulse, the will, in free mind, is self limited. In impulse, the will is not free, since its impulse and its object which determine it are something other than itself, whereas in free mind, the will is its own subject and so it is self-determined and also infinite. The free mind marks the end of the realm of the Subjective Spirit and the beginning of the realm of the Objective Spirit.

Section B
OBJECTIVE SPIRIT

As we have seen in Section-A, the Subjective Spirit with its last category, namely, free will, could not attain the state of universal satisfaction. So it externalizes or 'utters' itself in the form of the Objective Spirit which comprises the institutions* of law and the individual and social morality. Accordingly, the sphere of Objective Spirit is divided into the triad, viz , abstract or formal right, subjective morality and social ethics.

(i) *Abstract or Formal Right*

The abstract rights are those which apply to human beings considered abstractly, i.e., simply as persons and not as

---

* Hegel contends that the institutions found in the realm of Objective Spirit are not mere 'inventions' of man but the essential and necessary forms of Reason as the Objective Spirit. They are not human devices of expedience or convenience of seeking individualistic and unessential ends but rational manifestations of the Absolute which serve the universal and essential purposes of humanity. They are Spirit solidified in the world. It is a rational necessity that there should be the institutions of property, law, government, family, etc.

citizens of the state.** Hegel treats the institutions of property, contract and the punishment of wrong as the abstract rights. The institution of property gives a person the right to own the impersonal things. A person is free whereas a thing is unfree. So the former has necessarily a right to possess the latter. The person is an end and the object is his means. Hegel says, "Everyone has the right to make his will the thing or to make the thing his will or in other words to destroy the thing and transform it into his own, for the thing, as externality has no end in itself, it is not infinite self-relation but something external to itself."[14] The right to contract is the right of a person to withdraw his will from the object. That is, a person has right not only to possess the object but also to relinquish his right over it by transferring it to others.[15] The right of contract has its sub-categories, namely, contract of gifts, contract of exchanges, and contract of guarantees. Under these, Hegel deals with various topics like honesty, fraud, crime and punishment, the details of which are unnecessary.

Then the category of abstract right with last category of punishment passes on to the category of morality. Morality is not the outward thing like property but an affair of individual's inward conscience. It implies the harmony between

---

** According to Hegel, abstract right does not apply to animals. Animals may have consciousness but they are not persons, since they are not self-conscious. So, they do not have rights. It is only the persons who have rights and duties to each other.

14. Hegel, *Philosophy,of Right*, Translated by T.M. Knox, Clarendon Press, London, First ed. 1958, Reprint, 1967. p. 236 Addition.

15. Ibid., pp. 51-60.

the individual and the universal will. It is what the individual ought to be. It is the individual being in accord with the universal. Morality has three sub-divisions : (1) purpose, (2) intention and well-being and (3) goodness and wickedness. The category of purpose states that only the purposive action comes under moral consideration. That is, an individual cannot be held responsible for the action which is not done on purpose. Self-determination is the foundation of morality. And there is no infringement of self-determination if an action is not done on purpose. A person is held responsible only for what is done in his purpose.[16] Intention is the essential nature of the act willed in full awareness of its necessary consequences.[17] Moral agent ought to know the necessary consequences of his action. For instance, an individual holding a pistol to a man's head knows the necessary consequences of the latter's death, if the trigger is pulled. Well-being is that wherein the consequence of an act are comprehended for the personal as well as for the general good. For instance, an individual like poet in writing poetry for money and fame may also seek a universal end of giving pleasure to all through his poetry.[18] The category of intention and well-being proceeds to the category of goodness and wickedness. Goodness is the unity of the individual will with the universal will. It is the notion of the will which is universality. It is the notion which the will ought to be. The state of goodness is the universality of the will which is reason itself. "The good is the Idea as the unity of the concept of the will with the particular will...The good is thus freedom realized, the absolute end and aim of the world."[19] Wickedness happens to be when the individual will

16. Ibid., pp. 79-83.
17. Ibid., p. 81.
18. Ibid., p. 86.
19. Ibid.

opposes itself to the universal will. While goodness is the universal and necessary will of reason, wickedness is the self-will of whim and caprice. The aim of wickedness is governed by one's own ends whereas the aim of goodness is governed by the law. And the will that wills rationality is good will. The good will is reasonable will which wills reason to be done in the world. Now the abstract right proceeds to the category of subjective morality.

(ii) *Subjective Morality*

In subjective morality, the individual with his self-determining rational will acts without the help of any external agency. Here, the 'good' lies in one's own consciousness which is autonomous and infinite. Here, Hegel emphasises the rational consistency without deducing any positive duties from reason which is goodness. The subjective morality, according to Hegel, is one-sided for it is confined to the individual alone. It is half truth and may lead to capricious self-will. Therefore, the subjective morality necessarily passes on to social morality. In social morality, Hegel conceives of ethical systems or institutions which are the identity of the subjective and objective good. The institutions are the good will or reason in action. They are universal will actualised or reason objectified. They embody the true self of the subject which is free and autonomous. The institutions do not curtail individual freedom. Freedom is not the autonomous principle of individual freedom. The institutions with their laws are the embodiments in objectivity of the individual's rational or good will. Thus, in obeying the institutions one obeys only oneself. Hegel maintains that the laws of the institutions curtail not the rational and universal will but the natural and untrue will of individual whims and impulses.

(iii) *Social Ethics*

Social ethics manifests itself in the triad, viz., family, the civil society and the state. In the institution of family, rationality or universality exists in its immediacy and in the guise of the feeling of love.[20] It passes through three phases viz., (1) marriage, (2) the family means and (3) dissolution of the family. Marriage is love wherein the two persons renounce their personalities and be come one. It is not consciousness of the unity of the one with the other. It is not a contrivance for the benefit of the individuals who marry but an ethical bond and a necessary objectification of reason and the universal will. It is an ethical institution having an end which is higher than the pleasure of the individual. In marriage, the romantic feeling of being in love is subordinate to the universality of reason.[21] The institution of marriage passes to the category of the family means. Hegel treats family as one entity wherein the members are mutually dependent. Though it consists of many members, it amounts to only one person. So it has the property which is the possession of the whole family. It is this property that Hegel calls the family means which the head of the family viz., the husband holds in trust and by which the members of the family have the right to be maintained. Hegel holds that the access of the members of the family means is neither a previlege nor a favour done to them but their right based on season. It is their right with corresponding duties to their family. The family gets dissolved when the children get educated and become free and independent persons.[22] The family passes to the higher institution viz., civil society.*

---

20. Ibid., p. 110.
21. Ibid., p. 112.
22. Ibid., pp. 118-19.

* It should be noted that the origin of civil society, in the opinion of Hegel, is purely logical or rational but not historical.

Hegel is of the view that the notion of civil society is a logical deduction from the disruption of the family. In family, the members are not independent. They cannot treat themselves as ends but as means to the end called family. They become independent social atoms when the family is disrupted. Now each one treats himself as an end and the other as a means to his end. Thus each one depends upon all other which leads to an absolute inter-dependence of all upon all. It is this state of mutual dependence of each upon all others that Hegel calls civil society.[23]

The civil society passes through three stages viz., the system of wants, administration of justice, and police and corporation. In civil society, each person being independent, seeks to attain his private ends like food, drink, clothing, housing, etc. Hegel calls such ends wants,[24] for the achievement of which each one uses the other as a means. Thus the system of each one depending on the work of the other is the system of wants which consists of three subcategories viz., (1) mutual dependence, (2) labour and (3) wealth or capital. The system of wants necessitates mutual dependence which involves the universality of individual's work. That is, the individual working for his private end, cannot help working for others also. In aiming at his own ends, the individual aims at universal end. Labour is the means of moulding the natural material for the satisfaction of wants. It is the instrument that shapes ends out of crude matter.[25] And wealth is the property of the whole community. It is a general stock produced by and for all in producing for them-

23. Ibid., p. 122.
24. Ibid., p. 126.
25. Ibid., p. 128.

selves.[26] There are three classes of people depending upon the kind of wants they have, such as (1) the agricultural class, (2) the industrial and commercial class and (3) the universal class. The agriculture class lives in direct and immediate contact with nature. They receive what the nature gives. They just depend on nature without reflection.[27] The industrial and commercial class is reflection in Spirit. It depends more on work than nature.

The universal class is the governing class which works for the universal interests of society and state. It is dependent on the moment of reason.[28] The category of wants along with its sub-categories proceeds to the category of administration of justice, the second phase of civil society.

Administration of justice recognizes the mutual dependence of rights and duties and makes them laws which are universal. It establishes law in objectivity in the form of institutions.[29] Hegel holds that the laws are deduced from notion but not from expediency. They should be written in code and displayed in public places. They have to be protected and maintained in a world of capricious acts of particular wills. So there is a need for an authority like the court of justice which, according to Hegel, represents and vindicates the right and punishes the wrong in their universality. The category of the administration of justice passes to the category of police and corporation. Police is necessary for the regulation of the pursuits of person's well-being and for the protection of one individual from the other. The

26. Ibid., p. 130.
27, Ibid., p. 131.
28. Ibid., p. 132-134.
29. Ibid., pp. 134-38.

police has two sided duty to perform. One is the positive side of actualizing and institutionalizing the right of the individual. The other is the negative side of removing the casual contingencies and fortuitous hindrance from individual's right to his well-being.[30] Corporation is an institution established by a group of person having similar interests. The associations of this type are common in the world of commerce. Hegel maintains that though pursues its own interest, the corporation nevertheless, promotes the universal ends of society. The aims of corporation, being higher than those of an individual, raise the individual to the level of the universal.[31] The category of police and corporation passes to a more concrete category, namely, the state.

Dialectically viewed, the state is the synthesis of the family of internal relations and the civil society of external relations among persons. In terms of notional determinations, the state is the moment of individuality deduced from the sublation of the universality of family and the particularity of civil society. The state stands for the individual actualized and objectified. "It is a person, an organism which is self-differentiating in such a manner that the life of the whole appears in all parts. This means that the life of the parts i.e., the individuals, is found identical with the life of the whole, the state."[32] Since the state is implicitly the individual, it is not an alien power which suppresses the individual freedom; on the contrary, the state is a supreme embodiment of freedom. So, the individual, in being determined by the state, is determined by his essential self which is universal and true.

---

30. Ibid., p. 146.
31. Ibid., p. 152.
32. Stace, W. T., Loc. cit., p. 425.

The state is rational, since it is absolute and universal. "The state is the actuality of the ethical idea. It is ethical mind qua the substantial will manifested and revealed to itself, knowing and thinking itself, accomplishing what it knows and in so far as it knows it."[33]

The state is an embodiment of world-reason. In it, the freedom assumes the highest form of right. So it commands the individual to sacrifice his individuality and to obey its commands. Indeed, the individual can realize his freedom and individuality only by being a member of the state. Hegel says, "The state is absolutely rational in as much as it is the actuality of the substantial will which it possesses in the particular self-consciousness once that consciousness has raised to consciousness of universality. This substantial unity is an absolute, unmoved and in itself, in which freedom comes into its supreme right. On the other hand this final end has supreme right against the individual, whose supreme duty is to be a member of the state."[34]

The state is the union of the universal and the individual. It is the identity between the universal and the individual claims of well-being, since the individual is implicity universal and the state is the actualization of the freedom of the individual. That is, the actions of the individual lead to universal goals. So also the state, though suppresses the individual, stands for the well-being of the individual. However, the state is an organism constituted by the independent individuals of internal difference. The state maintains unity by administering its right on individuals. And the constitution is that which deals with the internal relation of the state to

33. Hegel, *Philosophy of Right*, Op. cit., p. 155.
34. Ibid., pp. 155-56.

its citizens. The constitution is a system which determines its activity in accordance with reason. "The constitution of the state is, in the first place, the organisation of the state and self-related process of its organic life, a process whereby it differentiates its moments within itself and develops them to self-subsistence."[35] The idea of the state passes through three stages: (1) the constitutional law or internal polity, (2) the international law and (3) the world history. The category of the constitutional law has three functions to perform, viz., the constitutional monarchy, the executive and the legislature.

It is only when the state is completely rational that it becomes a constitutional monarchy. The constitutional monarchy is the logical notion in actual existence. Hegel contends that the governments other than monarchy are imperfect. He says that the states governed by monarchs are superior to republics, since the monarch is one in whom all the activities of the state are co-ordinated by virtue of his birth and heredity. Hegel says, "The monarch, therefore, is essentially characterized as this individual, in abstraction from all his other characteristics, and this individual is raised to the dignity of monarchy in an immediate, natural fashion, i.e., through his birth in the course of nature."[36] Hegel pictures monarch as one who gives ultimate sanction to the laws; he treats the laws as flowing from the monarch who is the ultimate source of executive acts. From monarch Hegel passes to the executive. The function of the executive is the application of the laws that are universal to the individuals. It carries out the decisions of the monarch and helps in the

35. Ibid., p. 174.
36. Ibid., p. 184.

application and the maintenance of existing laws for the security of common ends. It is composed of civil servants and advisory officials. The category of executive passes to the category of legislature. The legislature is meant to extend and amend the already existent body of laws. Its function is to develop the laws to suit the new situations. "Legislative business is more precisely determined, in relation to private individuals, under these two heads : (a) provision by the state for their well-being and happiness, and (b) the extraction of service from them."[37] The legislature proceeds to the category of international law.

The state is an organic unity but not a mere aggregate of parts. It is a single sovereign being having two sides viz., (1) internal and (2) external. The internal side has already been dealt with under the category of 'internal polity.' The external aspect of the state deals with its relations with other states of its kind. The international law is constituted by the external relations that are recognized to be universalized. The relations between two states is similar to the relations between the persons in civil society. Each state is equally independent. None has authority over the other. So the international law protects the state's fundamental right of being sovereign. It ordains that the states continue to recognize one another as independent even at the time of war. The actuality of international law owes its existence to different states which are equally sovereign. The state is mind in its substantive rationality and immediate actuality. The state is therefore an absolute power on earth. The international law gives this truth the form of an ought-to-be. It helps forming treaties between the states without any disturbance to their sovereignty. "The fundamental proposition of international law (i.e., the universal law which ought to be absolutely valid between states, as distinguished from the

37. Ibid., p. 194.

particular content of positive treaties) is that treaties, as the ground of obligations between states, ought to be kept."[38] The international law allows war between the states whenever necessary. War is inevitable when the two states disagree on a particular will. The states find themselves in war, when there is a breach of treaty or an injury to the honour and autonomy of the state. Hegel observes : "It follows that if states disagree and their particular wills cannot be harmonized, the matter can only be settled by war."[39] He is of the view that war contains an element of necessity within itself. It would be unphilosophical if war is regarded as an evil and an accident caused by injustice and passion for power.[40]

Hegel contends that war has within itself an ethical moment, for it preserves the morality of people by subjugating them to obey the sovereignty. "War has the higher significance that by its agency, as I have remarked elsewhere, 'the ethical health of peoples is preserved in their indifference to the stabilization of finite institutions; just as the blowing of the winds preserves the sea from the foulness which would be the result of prolonged calm, so also corruption in nations would be product of prolonged, let alone 'perpetual' peace."[41] The category of international law proceeds to the category of world history.

The world history is the succession of the stages of universal idea in the Idea of states. Hegel says, "Each of its stages is the presence of a necessary movement in the Idea of the world mind, and that movement attains its absolute

38. Ibid., p. 213
39. Ibid., p. 214
40. Ibid., p. 209
41. Ibid., p. 210

right in that stage."[42] The world-history is not one of chance or blind fate. It is not a mere happening of contingent events. It is the movement of eternal Reason or Idea. Hegel says, "World history is the necessary development, out of the concept of mind's freedom alone, of the moments of reason and so of the self-consciousness and freedom of the mind. This development is the interpretation and actualization of the universal mind."[43] Hegel says that the Idea embodied in the world history is world spirit. The world-spirit in the form of world-history is the final tribunal of the nations. The verdict of all nations is found in the fate which awaits them in the development of world-history. The world-history is a court of judgment which determines the nation's destiny. Its judgment is not one of caprice or might but an exhibition of the historical inevitability.

Section C
ABSOLUTE SPIRIT

As it is already seen, the Subjective and Objective Spirits are the two opposite extremes limiting each other. They are absolutely independent and different from each other. The Absolute Spirit is the concrete reality which transcends the division between them. It is an actual consciousness which is neither purely personal nor purely impersonal. It is both consciousness of an individual and consciousness of the object. It is the absolute identity of the subject and the object. It is the mind which realizes whatever is opposed to it as nothing but itself. For it, the entire physical and non-physical world is nothing other than itself. It is all reality and all being. "Spirit, therefore, has for its object in this sphere,

42. Ibid., p. 217
43. Ibid., p. 216

nothing else than spirit itself. Absolute Spirit, therefore, is the spirit's contemplation of itself."[44]

Hegel holds that the Absolute Spirit is the knowledge of the Absolute by human being. since the Spirit exists only in human consciousness.* Hegel equates the self-knowing Absolute Spirit with the essential content of the human mind, which is freedom. The freedom of the mind is Absolute in the sense that it is devoid of all otherness. It has no opposite which determines it. Absolute Spirit is freedom which is infinite and self-determined. Hegel equates the Absolute Spirit with God, since it is endowed with all the qualities that God is endowed with. The Absolute Spirit expresses itself in three forms viz., art, religion and philosophy.

(i) *Art* : As we have already seen in the previous chapters, the general principle of Hegelian dialectic is that the Idea manifests, firstly, in its immediacy. In the realm of art, form and beauty are taken as the immediate modes of the Absolute. The form is the guise of external sense-object through which the Absolute manifests. And beauty is the shining of the Absolute through the veils of the world of sense-objects. Art is divided into three types viz., (1) the idea of artistic beauty or the ideal, (2) the development of the ideal into the particular forms of arts and (3) the system of the individual or particular arts. Beauty is sensuous in the sense that it essentially exists through an actual thing present to the senses like a chair, a building, a statue, the sound of music,

44. Stace, W. T., Loc. cit., p. 440

* For Hegel, the terms 'Spirit' and 'Absolute' are synonymous. So Absolute Spirit is the knowledge of the Spirit by Spirit and knowledge of the Absolute by the Absolute.

etc. But a mere mental image of a sensuous object in its abstraction is not beautiful. It becomes beautiful only when the mind perceives the Absolute through it. The Absolute Idea becomes the ideal, the beautiful, only when it is perceived through the sensuous world.[45]

According to Hegel, beauty and truth are identical, since they together constitute the absolute Idea. At the same time they are distinct, since the former is apprehended by the senses whereas the latter by pure thought.

Hegel holds that the form of the sensuous object through which the Idea gets apprehended is a unity of parts. This unity is not mechanical but organic in nature. It is not a mere aggregate, like a heap of stones in which each part is independent. On the contrary, the unity of sensuous object is such that its parts have no meaning except as members of the whole, like a hand which has no being apart from the entire body. He says "The beautiful object, e.g., the work of art, is essentially an organism."[46]

Beauty has two important forms, viz., (1) nature and (2) art. As already mentioned, nature is the Idea in its otherness. It is beautiful, since the Idea is implied in it.[47] Its beauty varies depending upon the degree of the manifestation of the Idea. Accordingly, there are three levels of beauty in nature. First, Idea in nature appears so sunk in externality as to be invisible; e.g., heap of stones which can be separated from one another. It is the lowest level of beauty and so

45. Hegel, *Aesthetics—Lectures on Fine Art*. Translated by T. M. Knox, Clarendon Press, Oxford. 1975, Vol. I, pp. 106ff
46. Stace, W.T., Loc. cit., p. 444
47. Hegel, *Aesthetics—Lectures on Fine Art*. Op. cit., p. 116.

scarecely beautiful. Second, the Idea appears in somewhat higher form than the former, e.g., the solar system. In it, there is an interdependence of the parts (planets) upon one another. Here the Sun acts as principle of unity, but the unity of the system is governed only by mechanical laws. Here, the unity is only an ideal one, for the Sun remains to be a separate material object from the other planets. Third, the Idea in nature appears in the form of living beings or life wherein the unity is organic, e.g., plants, animals and human beings. Here all the parts of a living organism are bound in an ideal unity. The part becomes meaningless when separated from the whole, e.g., a branch or a limb cut off from the tree or body, ceases to be a branch or a limb. It is in this phase that beauty is expressed in its true sense.[48]

Hegel is of the view that the beauty in nature is not perfect, since it does not possess the necessary qualities, viz., infinitude and freedom. The plants, animals and human beings do determine themselves. But at the same time, they are determined by their environment, needs and compulsions. To be precise, all that is in nature is unfree and finite. So the beauty of nature is essentially defective.* So the Idea of beauty in nature progresses itself to the level of the Idea of beauty in art.

Art is the creation of beauty by the Spirit. The subject that deals with the beauty of art is aesthetics. Hegel says that every work of art has two distinct sides, viz., (1) subjectivity

---

48. Stace, W.T., Loc. cit., p. 444.

* In treating the beauty of nature as inferior to the beauty of art, Hegel seems to have been very much under the influence of his notion of the supremacy of Reason. Critics of Hegel hold that Hegel is hasty in giving a low place to the beauty of nature.

or unity, (2) objectivity or plurality. One is of content and the other is of form. The former contains the spiritual significance and inner meaning of the latter whereas the latter represents the sensuous or the material form through which the subject reveals itself.[49] The Idea work of art is that wherein the content and form are in perfect union. Hegel divides art into three fundamental types basing on the different relations between the content and the form viz., (1) the art wherein form predominates over content, (2) the art where there is perfect balance between content and form and (3) the art wherein content predominates over form. Hegel equates the three types of art with the symbolic (earliest), the classical (medieval) and the romantic (modern) arts respectively. In symbolic art, the symbol is the medium through which a meaning is suggested without expression. In it, the symbol is the material form whereas the significance of symbol is the content. Hegel is of the view that symbolic art is mysterious and problematic, since the symbol cannot express the entire significance for which it stands. The symbol may be taken by different people to mean differently. So Hegel calls it "a paradise of riddles and problems."[50] Hegelis of the view that in Hinduism the realization of the contradiction between the content and form is unconsciously felt and the union between them is accomplished in purely sensuous, grotesque, monstrous and distorted shapes. "Among the ancient Hindus the separation was vaguely felt ....The cow, the ape, the serpent are worshipped as being varitably God."[51] The Egyptian art, according to Hegel, exhibits a higher stage of symbolism. It is more genuine symbolism, since the separation between the divine and sensuous is more clear. The Egyptian legends like the phoenix, the pyramids, the mammon statues and the temples represent the somewhat clear separation between the content and form of the work of art. Hegel believes that the art of the sublime as developed by

49. Hegel, *Aesthetics—Lectures on Fine Art*, Op. cit., p. 153.
50. Stace, W.T., Loc. cit., p. 453
51. Ibid., p. 454.

the Hebrew poets and prophets reveal the completely deliberate separation of the content and form. The sublime is entirely different from the beautiful. In it, the Absolute is conceived as the supreme reality and the phenomena as essentially fleeing. "The sublime is the attempt to express the infinite, without being able to find any sensuous medium which is adequate to express it—so that it remains at last the unspeakable, the unutterable......, the two sides being thus in full and harmonious accord."[52] Hegel says that the kindred symbolic art forms like the fable, the allegory, the parable, and the didactic poem represent the complete dissolution of the symbolic type of art, since in them the separation between the content and form is carried to the extent of breaking the link between them. The symbolic art is abstract in the sense that its content is not revealed either in particularity or individuality. In it, the content remains completely external to the art. The content is not a concrete universal, for it does not embody itself in individual forms. Thus, the symbolic art passes to the classical art wherein the Absolute is viewed not as a bare abstraction but grasped as the concrete. Hegel takes Greek art as an example of classical art. He says that Greek people have treated their God as anthropomorphic but not as an empty being. Their God is not an empty universal but spiritual individuality wherein the content and form are one. Hegel maintains that anthropomorphism, in which the divine embodies itself in concrete human form, is best suited to be the dwelling place of Spirit. Here man sees the Absolute in himself. Hegel treats the Greek sculpture as par excellence the classical art. "The essential notion of the classical type of art is that in it content and form are in perfect agreement and balance."[53] However, the classical art is finite and

52. Ibid., p. 457.
53. Ibid., pp. 459-60

unfree, for it is expressed only in particularity which is sensuous. So the Spirit does not remain at the level of classical art but passes to romantic type of art. In romantic art, the Spirit drops its veil of material embodiment and expatiates within its own subjectivity. So the subject matter of the romantic art is the inward life of Spirit.[54] In it, the Spirit completely predominates the form and grasps its own nature clearly. Dialectically viewed, the Spirit not only reposes blissfully in the universality of its subjectivity but also rends itself into two. It is not only in division and conflict within itself but also in the complete unity with itself. The unity of the Spirit is not born of inaction but won out of the heart of conflict with itself. "The inner conflict of Spirit with itself, its alienation from itself and its ultimate self-reconciliation, become the content of romantic art."[55]

Hegel holds that the romantic art of mediaeval period depicts the Spirit only in the form of conflict. It merely shows the Spirit as being torn. But Spirit becomes truly Spirit only when it splits itself into two and again becomes one. The unity, the Spirit attains after its division into itself and the spiritual other, is concerete. Hegel takes the art of Christendom as the example of romantic art. It is in Christian art that the conflict and triumph of the Spirit are clearly reflected. In it, the division and reconciliation of Spirit are envisaged as the life, death and resurrection of Christ. In it, the story of Christ represents the Absolute as concrete Spirit. Here the divine, the Absolute Spirit is depicted in flesh and blood.

The romantic art proceeds to the particular art which are of three types, viz., (1) the symbolic art of architecture,

54. Hegel, *Aesthetics—Lectures on Fine Art*, p. 519
55. Stace, W.T., Loc. cit., p. 463.

(2) the classical art of sculpture and (3) the romantic art of painting, music and poetry. In the symbolic art of architecture, the Idea gets expressed in the symbolic building which exists independently of the Idea.[56] The symbolic building has no purpose other than symbolizing some abstract idea. Hegel takes the tower of Babel as an example. The tower has not served any purpose except symbolizing the idea of the unity of the people who built it. So the tower is entirely an independent work of art. The symbolic architecture passes to the classical architecture. Unlike the symbolic art of architecture, the classical architecture is dependent in the sense that its works have a purpose other than symbolizing the idea.[57] For example, the Greek temples. They serve the purpose of providing an abode for the idol of the God. They are used as the places of worship. "These temples are not, primarily, symbolical of anything. They are wholly determined by their central Idea, which is to provide an enclosure and suitable environment for the statue of the God."[58] The classical architecture passes to the romantic architecture. Just as in the general type of romantic art, the essence of romantic architecture is the predominance of spirituality or content over form. In it, the subjectivity is completely cut off from the world. The Gothic Churches of modern Europe are the examples of this romantic architecture. The total withdrawal of the spirit from the form is represented in the construction of these Churches.[59] "The pillars are not outside but inside. The whole is entirely enclosed, forming an abode of the soul shut

---

56. Hegel, *Aesthetics—Lectures on Fine Art*, Op. cit., Vol. II, p. 635 ff.
57. Ibid., pp. 660-63.
58. Stace, W.T., Loc. cit., p. 469.
59. Hegel, *Aesthetics—Lectures on Fine Art*, Op. cit., pp. 684ff.

off in self-seclusion from the outside world. The Sun only enters in a glimmer through the stained glass windows. Every-one comes and goes, prays upon his knees and moves away. All kinds of religious acts are going on at the same time."[60] The romantic art of architecture passes to the concept of sculpture.

As we have seen already, architecture uses crass matter, like stone, as its medium whereas sculpture uses organic matter as its medium. Sculpture uses spiritualized matter or subjectivity as its medium. It expresses subjectivity especially, in the form of human shape.[61] It considers human body as its adequate mode of presentments. It is in human body which is purely sensuous that the content and form can be unified in perfect equipoise. It depicts Spirit in its undisturbed repose and universality, and excludes the violent agitations of the Spirit, e.g., the statues of the Greek Gods. The statues represent the immortality of the Spirit. They depict the lofty qualities like, fortune, love, justice, etc., and delineate the permanent and substantial features of human character such as goodness, honesty, courage, intelligence. The passing phases of human emotions like anger, surprise cannot be the suitable subject matter of this sculpture. "Mere idiosyncrasies of expression, mere caprices of action, all the more subjective and purely personal states of the soul, must be excluded. It is for this reason that the glance of the eye is absent in statuary of the best type, although, it is present in painting. For it is only in romantic art that the subjective depths of soul life can be delineated."[62] The classical art of sculpture

60. Stace, W. T., Loc. cit., p. 470

61. Hegel, *Aesthetics—Lectures on Fine Art*, pp. 702-703.

62. Stace, W. T. Loc. cit., p. 472.

passes to the romantic art.* The romantic art is divided into painting, music and poetry.

As it has been mentioned already, the principle of romantic art is that there is in the withdrawal of Spirit from the sensuous world. This principle is accomplished in the form of the negation of space or dissipation of the sensuous embodiment. This is shown in painting, the first type of romantic art. Painting does not need as its medium crass matter existing in reality. Instead, it takes as its basis only the appearnce of the solid matter. The sensuous side of painting is more mental than material.[63] It creates illusion through the differentiation of color and light. Hegel says that illusion in painting is not a defect but a mark which renders painting superior to sculpture. Painting as romantic art is not confined to the universal and permanent traits of human character, since subjectivity is predominant in it. It also deals with individual peculiarities like caprice, idiosyncrasies etc. However, painting is limited, since it can only exhibit a single moment in time. "It is not in itself, as both music and poetry are, a process in time which can develop the various stages of an action."[64] Painting proceeds to music.

Music as romantic art does not appeal to the sense of sight but to the sense of hearing. It negates space altogether and so exists only in time. Therefore, it is purely subjective.[65]

---

* Hegel has not sufficiently dealt with the symbolic and romantic sculpture, but the ommission of their discussion does not stand in the way of our understanding of Hegel's account of aesthetics.

63. Hegel, *Aesthetics—Lectures on Fine Art*, Op. cit., pp. 799 ff.
64. Stace, W.T., Loc. cit., p. 472.
65. Hegel, *Aesthetics—Lectures on Fine Art*, Op. cit., pp. 888 ff.

The substance of music, viz., the tone does not have objectivity and permanence of subsistence like the substances of architecture and painting, viz., status and picture respectively. There is no separation of object and subject in music. It is the most emotional, since it penetrates into the core of the soul. "In emotion this separation is absent. The soul is absorbed in its object, is interwoven with the object in a thoroughghing identity."[66]

Music is not a mere medley of sounds. Music becomes art only when the soul introduces the ordered relation, among the various sounds. Rhythm, time-beats and conformity play an important role in music. It is out of this symmetry in sounds that the ego finds profound satisfaction in music. According to Hegel, the time-beat in music has the philosophical basis. Music has firm grip on the soul. The soul finds in music the absolute counterpart of itself viz., "a bare unity, sundering itself, and again returning into unity and identity with itself."[67] Music proceeds to poetry.

In poetry, the sound becomes a word. The word is an arbitrary sign for an idea. The image in poetry possesses the feature both of content and form, since it belongs to subjectivity and also to individuality. Since language is capable of expressing anything that human mind is capable of thinking, poetry is not confined to a particular phase of Spirit. In poetry, there is the unity and the identity of the universal and the particular. It holds the abstract and concrete in unity. Hegel says, "poetry, the art of speech, is the third term, the totality, which unites in itself, within the province of the spiritual inner life and on a higher level two extremes, i.e., the visual arts and music."[68]

---

66. Stace, W.T., Loc. cit., p. 475.
67. Ibid., p. 476.
68. Hegel, *Aesthetics—Lectures on Fine Art*, Op. cit., p. 960.

Poetry is divided into three main divisions; (1) epic (2) lyric and (3) dramatic. Hegel is of the view that the epic poem must be objective in the sense that is should describe only the particular action done by particular persons.[69] The poet should only be a narrator of the objective world of persons, things and events e.g., Homer's Iliad and Odyssey. Homer has described in his Iliad, the wrath of Achilles and in Odyssey he has described hero's adventures which arise purely from external circumstance as well as from his peculiar character. Epic poetry passes to the lyric poetry. Contrary to the epic poetry, the principle of lyrical poetry is subjectivity.[70] Here the poet though concentrates on his own soul-life he appeals to the human heart in general. It passes to the dramatic poetry which combines the principles of subjectivity and objectivity of the work of art.[71] It is subjective in the sense that it develops outward action through the inward soul-life. It is objective in the sense that it places before us a definite series of events of the outward world. So it is also the unity of the lyric and epic poetry. It is the universal art of the spirit which is free in itself and not bound for its realization to external sensuous material. The development of art comes to an end in dramatic poetry which marks the transition of Idea to a higher phase, viz., religion.

(ii) *Religion* : As we have seen already, art is an inadequate cognition of the Absolute Spirit, for it apprehends the Absolute Spirit in the form of sense-objects. The romantic art contains within itself a contradiction, because instead of confining itself to the sense-object relation, it takes the inward life of the soul or the subjectivity as its subject matter. Thus,

69. Ibid., pp. 1040 ff.
70. Ibid., p. 1113.
71. Ibid., p. 1158 ff.

romantic art transcends the realm of art completely and enters the realm of religion. "It is, infact, a transitional stage, in which spirit is already beginning to leave the sphere of art behind and pass into the higher sphere of religion."[72]

Religion is an intermediate stage between art and philosophy. In it, the Absolute is apprehended neither as purely sensuous nor as purely rational but as partly sensuous and partly rational. Hegel calls this intermediate form of Absolute Spirit the absolute vorstellung, which means pictorial thought. Religion is pure thought clothed in sensuous imagery. It is the figurative existence of rational truth. As Hegel puts it, "The vorstellung is, like the mental image, purely inward, but is in addition a definite step towards the universality of thought. It is in this respect that religion constitutes an advance upon art, and solves, at least proximately, too contradiction immanent in art."[73] Hegel speaks of two phases of religion viz., (1) religion in general and (2) definite religion.

Religion in general is neither accidental nor a human contrivance for convenience but a necessary work of Reason. It exhibits the three notional determinations, viz., universality, particularity and individuality. The universal, in religion, is God. The particular is the human mind which is in alienation from God. Hegel is of the view that alienation of the human mind from God appears as sin and misery. The individuality is reconciliation of the particular person with the universal. It implies the union of man with God. The separation and union are accomplished through the element of worship which is an essential aspect of religion in general. Here the human mind knows that it is itself all reality which is the

---

72. Stace, W. T., Loc. cit., p. 462.
73. Ibid., p. 488.

Absolute.* However, religion in general is one-sided. It is of mere subjectivity. Therefore, it passes to definite religion which is religion in its objectivity. It is the existence of religion in the form of the various religions of the world. Apart from its subjective and objective aspects, religion necessarily passes through three great phases, viz., (1) natural religion, (2) the religion of spiritual individuality and (3) the absolute religion.

To Hegel, the natural religion is that in which Spirit has not yet gained mastery over nature. Here, the spirit is recognised not as absolute and supreme but as being within the power of nature. The natural religion passes through three stages, viz., (1) immediate religion or magic, (2) the religion of substance and (3) the religion in transition. In the immediate religion, the distinction between God and man does not exist. Here everything is particular and the universal is not yet recognised. "There is nothing but this tree, this river, this animal this man. Hence man does not distinguish himself from nature. He is merely a unit, like any other unit, amid a chaos of particular objects."[74] In the immediate religion, though the Spirit is under the power of nature, it can, at the same time, in the form of 'I' or particular 'ego' appear as

* To Hegel, Philosophy of identifying the human mind with everything is not pantheistic. Pantheism is the thesis that every individual object, including the individual man, even in its immediacy and particularity, is God. But Hegel identifies the world of objects with God only when the particular human mind surpasses immediacy, particularity and finiteness. The individual mind has to give up all its selfish impulses and realise the universal mind which is its inner core. It is only then that it becomes one with everything.

74. Ibid., p. 492.

being superior to nature. That is, the Spirit, by its sheer will-power, can command nature. It can have power over the clouds, the storms, the waters etc. This is what Hegel calls magic. However, the Spirit is regarded as being in bondage to nature even in magic, for the impulses and passions which control nature in magic belong to the natural but not to the spiritual or rational side of man. Here the Spirit exists in the 'form' of dim consciousness but not consciousness as notion. So the immediate religion proceeds to the religion of substance.

In the religion of substance, the God is conceived as a pure abstract and universal substance without any particular content. Man and the world are conceived as particularities completely dependent upon the substance. Everything arises out of and disappears into the substance. That is, the substance "produces all finite existences as transitory and unessential modifications of itself."[75] There are three grades of the religion of substance, viz., the Chinese religion, Hinduism and Buddhism. In Chinese religion, God is conceived not only as an empty, undifferentiated being, but also as an empirical consciousness. Here, God is both a universal being and a particular spirit who rules not only particular individuals, and elements of nature but also the spirits of the dead. In Hinduism, the concept of God* as substance is wholly abstract and undetermined without any differentiation within itself. It is without form and name. It is independent and beyond personification. It is called Brahman. Everything other than Brahman is unreal, accidental and dependent on Brahman. Hegel is of the view that though Brahman is,

75. Ibid., p. 493.

* Hegel's account of God in Hindu religion reveals Advaita view only.

at times, spoken as having personality, it is still only a substance but not spirit. It is not concrete but abstract and empty. So it cannot produce the particular existents viz., all beings, all worlds, all men, all gods, as the Absolute Spirit can. "It does not genuinely produce them out of itself and then again restore its own unity by taking them back into itself."[76] Here the Absolute is only a chaos of disconnected forms. It is not governed and connected by Reason. Hegel holds that Hinduism presents a chaotic world-view. Its monotheism coupled with its grotesque polytheism leaves the particular existents in an uncontrolled confusion. Hegel says that though notion is at work in the Trimurthi concept of Hinduism, it cannot be identified with the Christian Trinity which is the perfect realization of notion in the religious sphere. He maintains that if the Hindu concept of Trimurti is to be equated with Christian Trinity, Brahma, Vishnu and Shiva should be treated as the universal, the particular and the individual respectively. Shiva should be treated as the unity of the universal Brahman and the particular Vishnu. But, Hegel contends that the Hindu Trimurtis are three entirely different manifestations. The virtues of Christian religion are foreign to Hinduism. In Hinduism, Brahman is an abstract substance and the element of worship is meant to unite oneself with Brahman who is contentless. Hegel contends that salvation does not lie in the worship of making oneself abstract and contentless. In true religion which conceives God as Spirit, salvation is attained through the concrete work of "striving after universal ends, in morality, in the state, and in religion."[77]

Hegel holds that Buddhism too like Hinduism is inadequate, since it also recognises only substance as God.

76. Ibid., p. 495.
77. Ibid., p. 497.

Here, God is the substance which is pure non-being. Worship is aimed at the attainment of nothingness by the suppression of all desires. Worship also implies the embodiment of substance in a particular empirical consciousness of the Buddha or the Dalailama who is worshipped as the absolute power.* The religion of substance passes to the religion in transition.

In the religion in transition, the concept of God is shown as evolving from substance to Spirit which is not yet completely and definitely concrete. Hegel takes Zorastrianism, the Syrian religion and the Egyptian religion as the religions in transition.

In Zorastrianism God is undermined by recognizing as the power of substance but not Spirit. Here, God is not fully undetermined because it is qualified by good, viz., Ormazd. Here the good is still abstract. It has its opposite, the evil, viz., Ahirman, the good, being abstract, does not produce the evil, since the evil is only the other of the Ormazd. The evil is itself an absolute and independent being like the good. So the good and evil are absolutely opposite to each other. This represents dualism without any possibility of unity. "There is division, opposition, strife. But what is essential to the idea of spirit, namely, that this division, this strife, should be within itself, is lacking. The Good here wages war with a wholly external principle."[78]

Further, Hegel contends that the Ormazd and Ahirman of Zorastrianism are not genuinely spiritual individuals. Their

---

* Hegel's knowledge of Buddhism is deficient. He seems to have been ignorant of Hinayana Buddhism, which is considered to be the original doctrine of Buddha and does not treat Buddha or Lama as God. In it, there is no place for worship. However, for the sake of dialectical continuity, we have furnished the above Hegel's account of Buddhism as religion.

78. Ibid., p. 501.

personification is only superficial. They are not persons in flesh and blood. Moreover, they are, at times, identified with light and darkness respectively. Therefore the Zorastrianism is still within the religion of nature. The Zorastrianism passes to the Syrian religion.

The defect in Zorastrianism is that the 'other' of the universal is only an external principle that falls outside the universal. The Syrian religion realises this defect by treating the 'other' as being within God himself. Here the division of strife between the universal and particular is within God himself. However, the strife, the essential element of Spirit, is represented only symbolically between the myths of Adonis, the God and phoenix, the bird. Therefore the Syrian religion passes to Egyptian religion.

In Egyptian religion, the Osiris, the God contains within itself the element of negation. Here, God negates himself by being killed by his opposite, viz., Typhon, the evil principle. The negation by death is internal, since the God rises again and becomes the lord of the living and of the spirits of the dead. This resurrection of God is the negation of the negation which is death. It is here, that the third moment of the notion takes place. It is through the negation of the negation that the division is bridged and conflict is resolved. "Spirit is the universal which, firstly, particularizes itself, negates itself, produces its opposite out of itself and then secondly, negates this negation, resumes its opposite in identity with itself."[79] Now the religion in transition comes to an end and passes on to the religion of spiritual individuality.

In the three phases of the transitional religion, according to Hegel, the Spirit appears in fragments and sensuous symbols. Here God is only an abstract substance and not a Spirit per-

79. Ibid., p. 502.

sonified in concrete reality. But in the religions of spiritual individuality, Spirit appears as a definite and concrete reality. It reaches the idea of personal-God who enters the world and takes part in its certainties such as politics, morals, agriculture, etc. Here God is perfect wisdom and the individual who is free and independent. Here the particular does not vanish in the universal but is allowed to go forth out of itself in freedom. Here, the religious life is not a withdrawal from the world but an active life of morality in the state. Hegel regards the Jewish, the Greek and the Roman religions as the religions of spiritual individuality.

In Jewish religion, God is one person viz., Johovah. The oneness of God is not the same as impersonal oneness of the Hindu religion. However, the oneness of God is un real, since the particular does not form part of Him. Secondly, God as Spirit should act in accordance with the ends. But here God being the only reality, there is no room for anything to serve as ends. God's end is only Himself and all other things are worthless. And worship is meant to concede one's nothingness before God. Here the attitude of man towards God is one of fear. So man is not free before God.[80] Thirdly, here God exists solely as Spirit and is conceivable only by thought. He is not represented in images and statues, for representation of God in zoolatry and idolatry is abominable. Hegel proceeds from Jewish religion to the Greek religion. He considers the Greek religion the religion of humanness, for in it, the God viz., Zeus, Appollo and Poscidon are human in the sense that they are not the personification of abstract principles but genuine persons. "Each is a living individuality with a wealth of character, a multiplicity of traits, not personifications of a single attribute."[81]

80. Ibid., p. 506.
81. Ibid., p. 507.

The Greek religion is a religion of free man. Here man is self-determined, independent and no longer negated by God. Instead, he is an essential manifestation of God. The relation of man to God is not one of fear. Greek Gods are friendly Gods. They are human and gracious. God and man are equal spirits. Here worship manifests in the form of festivals, processions, songs, plays, games and works of art. However, Hegel contends that there is an element of irrationality in Greek religion, since it accepts fate as the element of necessity which rules over even the Gods. Fate is abstraction without rational basis. So the Greek religion proceeds to Roman religion.

As we have seen already the Jewish God has only one end which is himself. The Greek gods being human in character, have many ends. They are finite beings with finite ends. But the Roman divinity combines both the qualities of the Gods of the Jewish and the Greek religions. That is, God in Roman religion is both a universal end and a particular end which belong to the world. Hegel equates the latter end with the state which is universal and brings all people under its power. "Jupiter Capitolinus is the embodiment of this idea. He has for his end, the universal sovereignty and dominion of the Roman people."[82] From the Roman religion thought proceeds to the revealed or the absolute religion, namely, the Christianity.

According to Hegel, Christianity is the only religion which fully accords with the notion of religion which is the manifestation of the Absolute in the form of thought. The truth of the true religion is determined by whether or not its inner thought content is found to be true after its figurative and sensuous form has been stripped off. Accordingly, in

82. Ibid., p. 508.

Christianity, the inner meaning and thought-content of figurative expressions like Father and Son, Creation, Heaven, the Fall are found to be identical with the principles of the only true philosophy, viz., Hegelianism. The content of Christianity and Hegelianism according to Hegel are the same but expressed in different forms. Philosophy expresses the absolute content in the absolute form which is pure thought, whereas Christianity expresses the same in the form of sensuous and pictorial thought which Hegel calls vorstellung. Indeed, Hegelianism is esoteric Christianity. Dialectically viewed, the concrete Spirit in the Christian vorstellung corresponds to the moments of the notion of Hegelianism. In Christian vorstellung the moments of the notion can be seen in the form of God as He is in his own self. Here God is an abstract universal prior to the creation of the world. Secondly, God as the abstract universal becomes the particular by creating the world of nature and people. Lastly, the particular, namely, the world returns to the universal and becomes the individual in the form of the Church. Hegel elucidates the three spheres of Christianity viz., the God, the World and the Church under three heads, viz., the kingdom of the Father, the Son and the Spirit.[83]

The Kingdom of the Father deals with the nature of God as he is in himself prior to the creation of the world. God, as such, is the Idea or the notion which is three-fold viz., universal, particular and individual. As the universal, God is the Father. As the universal produces the particular out of itself, so also God as universal begets the Son. And as the particular returns into the universal and becomes the individual, so also, the son returns to God and becomes the

83. Loewenberg, Jacob (ed), *Hegel Selections*, Charles Scribner's & Sons, New York, 1957, p. 290.

Holy Spirit. The three factors of the notion of God are not three parts of notion. Each is itself the notion, the God. The God as Father, is both the Son and the Holy Spirit. The Son is both the Father and the Holy Spirit. And the Holy Spirit is both the Father and the Son. Just as the Notion in Logic, God here contains three moments at the same time. This appears in Christianity as the doctrine of the Trinity. God is one and yet God is three persons—Father, Son and Holy Spirit. Each necessarily involves the other. The three are the entire Godhead. The category of the kingdom of the Father passes to the category of the kingdom of the Son.

The main triad of Hegel's dialectic is Idea—Nature-Spirit. Just as the Idea passes into Nature, so also God creates the world which gets reconciled to God again. Just as the Nature is the otherness of Idea, so also the world is the otherness of God. Just as there is the alienation between the Idea, the universal and the Nature, the particular, so also there is estrangement between God, the Father and Man, the Son. In Christianity this estrangement, according to Hegel, can be seen in the doctrine of the fall, which stands for man's separation from God. The doctrine of fall represents man's particularity and finitude as against God's universality and infinitude. But man overcomes his estrangement of particularity by returning to God in individuality wherein man is both the particular and the universal. In Christianity, the reconciliation or the unity between man and God can be seen, according to Hegel, in the doctrines of incarnation, the death of Christ, and His resurrection. God being the concrete universal enters into the finite world in flesh and blood.[84] God in person is Christ. He is finite and particular. But he reaches the extreme of finite and particularity and suffers death and resurrects as the Father. It is here, the reconciliation between the universal and the particular, God and Christ is complete. The kingdom of the Son passes to the kingdom of Spirit.

84. Ibid., pp. 290-91.

The kingdom of the Father is the Logical Idea and the kingdom of the Son is the Idea of Nature and the unity of the two is the kingdom of the Spirit. So the God as the Father and the God as the Son gets reconciled in the Spirit[85] which is represented by the Church in the world. The Church is the kingdom of God upon the earth of men. It is both the pure Spirit of God and also the community of men actually present in the world. Thus Hegel deals with religion as a whole in terms of the dialectical moments. He follows the historic evolution of religion passing through various stages which he depicts as necessary. Eventually, he arrives at Christianity and regards it as explicitly realizing the notion of religion. However, the development of the Idea as Spirit does not stop at religion, for religion, with its picture thought is not completely free from inconsisteneies. As Findlay puts, "Its speculative content will not always accord with its representational, quasi-empirical mode of statement. It must, therefore, press onward to Philosophy, in whose abstract conceptual medium it is alone possible to make the Idea a concrete achievement."[86] The category of religion passes to the category of philosophy.

(iii) *Philosophy* : Philosophy, according to Hegel, is the history of philosophical thought from Thales' to Hegel himself. Philosophy is the recaputulation of the reflective history of Spirit by itself. Hegel holds that the historical sequence of philosophical systems is not casual but a necessary development of the self-knowing Spirit. He maintains that the world-spirit does away with all its contingent and objective essence in the realm of philosophy only. And it is in his philosophy only that Spirit manifests itself as the Absolute. Here, philo-

85. Ibid., pp. 291-92.
86. Findlay, J.N., Loc. cit., p. 345.

sophy and Spirit are one and the same. Just as the Absolute Spirit is the totality of all its moments, so also Hegel's philosophy is the epitome of the truth of all previous philosophies. It sums up all previous stages of philosophy.[87] It is only in Hegel's philosophy that the mind is both the knower and the known. The knower, the subject and the known, the object are the Idea itself. It is here only that the gulf between the subject and the object has been absolutely and finally reconciled. The long course of mental discipline aimed at attaining the (knowledge of) Absolute ultimately finds complete fulfilment. The mind attains the knowledge of the Absolute in direct revelation of the Absolute Idea of Spirit.

Philosophy marks the end of all contingency and the beginning of necessity. Philosophy is the sphere where the world is comprehended not as vorstellung but as a necessary manifestation of the Spirit itself. In philosophy, Spirit is the world and vice versa. Here, everything is comprehended in its certainty. Hegel holds that philosophy is the self-knowledge of the Spirit as Absolute. "It is knowing itself in the shape of spirit, it is knowledge which comprehends through notions."[88]

It is to be noted that the Idea becomes an object of itself even in the realm of Logic. But the Idea as found at the end of Logic is only 'abstract' whereas Idea in philosophy is concrete. Philosophy itself is the Idea in concrete reality. It is the Idea completely realized in existence. Philosophy, according to Hegel, does not deal with determination that is non-essential. The abstract and the unreal are not its content. Its only content is what is real, what is life within itself and what is existence in its very notion. The end of philosophy

87. Ibid., p. 345.
88. Hegel, *The Phenomenology of Mind*, Op. cit., p. 798.

is the revelation of the depth of spiritual life which is Absolute Idea. Its goal is Absolute Idea or knowledge which is Spirit knowing itself as Spirit. Accordingly philosophic spirit is the comprehension of the purpose and the end of the world-process, viz., the revelation of the truth that everything is Spiritual or rational. Rational is divine and everything, being rational, is equally divine. Thus, in philosophy, the final stage of the phenomenology of mind, all that was hitherto regarded as relatively inward and immanent manifests itself in time and in Spirit's certainty of itself.[89]

To conclude, the aim of Hegel's philosophy is to comprehend the Absolute as a whole and in terms of necessity. The method, he adopts, is dialectical which passes through three important stages, viz., Logic, Nature and Spirit. The Absolute is the fundamental object in all the three stages. The three stages are the three stages of the Absolute. The first stage is Absolute as it is "in-itself," the second is the Absolute as it is "for-itself;" the third is the Absolute as it is "in and for-itself." That is Logic is the Absolute in its pure identity; Nature is the Absolute in its pure diversity; and Spirit is the Absolute in its identity and diversity; it is the Absolute as completely realized in human experience.

The entire system of Hegel's philosophy is a series of affirmations of the Absolute in the dialectical framework. Each affirmation is a partial definition of the Absolute; a partial definition is an abstract comprehension of the Absolute; it is only a relative affirmation of the Absolute. Thus, the dialectical development of Hegel's system is a contant cancellation of all the one-sided affirmations till the Absolute is realized as a whole. Hegel's philosophy is a process of the Absolute from abstract to concrete. It is a development from a lower to a higher degree of articulation of the nature of the Absolute.

89. Ibid., p. 800.

It is a growth from potentiality to actuality and from implicitness to explicitness.

Thus Hegel fulfils his ambitious task of explaining everything in the universe and universe as a whole. His system stands out prominently in the history of philosophy as the only one which encompasses all the spheres of human existence. At the same time, his philosophy—the dialectical scheme and treatment of the universe—has been subject to a severe criticism which we are going to consider in the next chapter.

CHAPTER V

EVALUATION

Hegel was a thinker who has occupied a pre-eminent place in the history of philosophy. He has exerted a lasting influence on human thought. The impact of his influence is such that his thought has inspired the highly original thinkers like Bradley in England, Royce in U.S., Croce and Gentile in Italy, Jean Hypolite in France and a host of other thinkers of Marxist and Existentialist trends. Similarly, Hegel's thought has given birth to various philosophical movements and counter movements.

He is an architect of an encyclopaedic system encompassing the logical, the natural and the spiritual aspects of human existence. His system presents a synthesis of human knowledge of thousands of years. It is an endeavour to accomplish the task of giving an integrated account of the universe in its entirety. The method that he has adopted is dialectic. Though Hegel's dialectic has been hailed as a potent method of describing reality, it is, at the same time, subjected to a severe criticism. It is, held that dialectic as a method is vague. The protean tricks through which Hegel operates dialectic makes its meaning and purpose teasingly obscure. And his discrepant account of it leaves us in a doubt whether dialectic can be characterized as a method at all.

Schopenhauer, an arch critic of Hegel observes that Hegel's dialectical philosophy sets out to be a science of 'pure' concepts but it generates them without recource to 'intuition.'* It produces misconceived thoughts about the world which pervert the mind of the young; it is a mere display of words which disgusts the reader with its abstractness; it is not aimed at truth at all but only concerned with mystifying the readers. He calls Hegel a dishonest charlatan who masquerading as a philosopher, casts a pernicious influence on German culture.[1]

Feurbach, who gave a materialistic turn to Hegel's idealism by replacing religion and theology by anthropology holds that Hegel's dialectic is an internal monologue by a speculative thinker, since it begins with the so called absolute and speculative truth, namely, "pure being" but not with the sensuous reality of the individual existence. Feurbach says that Hegel's dialectic ignores the empirical point of view which is more concrete and real than the speculative one. He maintains that the dialectical identification of the real and the ideal is not based on an earnest demonstration but accepted on faith. It is more a formal game than a dialectical necessity.[2]

Hegelian dialectic greatly influenced thinkers like Marx and Engels. Kantian dialectic is the basis of Hegelian dialectic

---

* Schopenhauer uses the term 'intuition' in totally different sense from that of Hegel. He uses it in the oriental sense of transcending the realm of reason, whereas Hegel uses it in Kantian sense of spatio-temporal attention filled with the certitude of reason.

1. Stephen Haulgate, *Hegel, Nietzsche and the Criticism of Metaphysics*, Cambridge University Press, 1986, p. 28.

2. Posaune, p. 81 Cf., John Edward Toews, *Hegelianism* path toward Dialectical Humanism, 1805-1841), Cambridge Univsrsity Press, 1980, p. 324.

which in turn forms the basis of Marxian dialectic Just as the Hegelian dialectic would not be possible without Kantian dialectic, Marxian dialectic would not have been there without Kantian dialectic. Hegel enhances the value of Kantian transcendental dialectic confined only to a set of cosmological ideas by applying it to the whole of universe. So also Marx makes Hegelian idealistic dialectic more fruitful by rending it materialistic. Marx accepts the dialectic process as the method of understanding history and thought. But he does not admit reason as the embodiment and the ultimate principle of reality. Marx holds that it is matter but not abstract reason or thought that is the basis of reality which is dialectical in nature. The fundamental reality, according to Marx, is not idea but matter which is all pervading. Thus Marx supplies a materialistic basis for the Hegelian dialectic and thus makes it stand on its head. He turns its right side up and discovers the rational kernal within the mystical shell.[3] Marx holds that the rational or the ideal is nothing more than the material world reflected in and translated by the human mind into forms of thought.[4] He maintains that the mind is the product of matter in dialectical motion; the appearance of mind is dependent on certain physical conditions. Its occurrence is purely identical with the operations in the physical nature. Thus Marx treats the laws of being as the basis of the laws of thought.

It is, therefore, clear that Marx does not simply put Hegel aside. On the contrary, he begins with Hegel's revolutionary method of dialectical evolution but he does not use it as is; he changes its content by adopting a thorough going

3. Marx, Karl, *Capital*, Progress Publishers, Moscow, 1977, Vol. I, p. 29.
4. Ibid., p. 25.

naturalism and achieves tremendous results in the field of social sciences. Marx says that the heart of Hegelian dialectical philosophy is nothing but "the speculative expression of the Christian—Germanic dogma of the opposition between spirit and matter, God and world."[5]

Engels too admits that the Hegelian dialectic comprehends the reality of the world in its entirety by bringing the opposite elements into internal harmony. He appreciates Hegel's discovery of three important dialectical laws, viz., (1) the law of the transformation of quantity into quality and vice versa, (2) the law of the interpenetration of opposites, and (3) the law of the negation of the negation.* He incorporates them in his dialectical treatment of social reality. But he contends that these laws are not idealistic or subjective but entirely objective in the sense that they are the essential laws of the objective viz., nature. Their reality lies not in thought but in matter.[6] And the Hegelian subjective laws are only the reflection of the objective laws of nature. Engels says, "Dialectics, so called objective dialectics, prevails throughout nature, and so called subjective dialectics, dialectical thought, is only the reflection of the motion through opposites which assert itself everywhere in nature and which by the continual

---

* The dialectical law of the transformation of quantity into quality and vice versa has been discussed on pages 32-34. The law of the interpretation of opposites has been discussed on pages 40, 41 & 42 and detailed account of the law of negation of negation has been considered on pages 52, 55 and 59.

5. Marx, Karl, *The Wholly Family*, Progress Publishers, Moscow, p. 186.

6. Engels, Frederick, *Dialectics of Nature*, ProgressPublishers, Moscow, p. 62.

conflict of the opposites and their final passage into one another, or into higher forms, determines the life of nature."[7]

Karl R. Popper, one of the chief critics of Hegel, attacks Hegelian dialectic on three counts. Firstly, Popper holds that Hegel's dialectical method suffers from a 'reinforced dogmatism.' Popper says that Hegel claims the credit of surpassing Kant's transcendental dialectic by extending the dialectical principle of contradiction not only to the noumena but also to the phenomena. Hegel maintains that Kant was dogmatic since Kant failed to treat contradiction as the truth of every facet of life. He holds that Kant could not comprehend the fact that all reality—noumena and phenomena—is of the nature of contradiction and could not grasp the inherent identity involved in codtradictions. But Popper maintains that real solution lies not in putting up with contradictions but in rejecting them, since it is logically absured to admit as true the two contradictory statements. Thus, if Kant was said to be a dogmatist, for having rejected rational metaphysics as meaningless, Hegel's attitude of putting up with contradictions and his ingeneous way of solving them is an extremely dangerous kind of dogmatism which he calls 'reinforced dogmatism' of making his method secure against all criticism.[8]

Secondly, Popper contends that Hegel's dialectic is not omnipresent. He refutes Hegel's claim that dialectic is the soul of the development of scientific knowledge. He says that the dialectical method may be successfully applied to the development of philosophical theories. It can very well

---

7. Ibid., p. 211.
8. Popper, Karl, R., *Conjectures and Refutations*, Routledge & Kegan Paul Ltd., London, 1981, p. 327.

comprehend the development of reason through history of philosophy. But it cannos be applied to the realm of science, for reasoning in science does not follow the dialectical law of contradiction. Scientific reasoning is intelligible within the realm of ordinary logic of dispensing with the knowledge that suffers from contradiction. He holds that the history of scientific theories may be described in terms of the dialectical reasoning but not the scientific reasoning itself.[9]

Thirdly, Popper is of the view that Hegel's over emphasis upon the role of reason suffers from panlogism of arguing that facts contradict each other since ideas in the realm of reason are contradictory. He denies Hegel's view that reason and reality are synonymous and ruled by the law of contradiction. He contends that contradiction may be the law of the abstract realm of reason but not of the factual world. The traditional law of contradiction reveals that facts can never contradict each other. In fact, the so called contradictions in the factual world are not real contradictions but only 'polarities.' For instance, Hegel may interpret the relation between positive and negative elements of electricity as contradictory. But Popper treats it as only 'polarity' which implies the necessary and mutual dependence of the two poles but not their contradiction. Thus Popper does not agree with Hegel's idea of identifying reason with reality and the consequent application of dialectic to the factual world. He therefore, condemns Hegel's dialectical philosophy as absurd, vague, elastic and an erroneous philosophical device which can justify all sorts of developments, even the contrary ones in the history of human thought.[10]

Findlay, an important exponent of Hegel's thought, is of the view that the triadic transition in Hegel's dialectic is

---

9. Ibid., p. 328.
10. Ibid., p. 329.

non-logical in the sense that it violates the important logical rule, namely, the law of the identity of opposites. He contends that the dialectical transition from category to category is of the nature of association based on experience but not on necessity. It is only a violent way of fitting the material drawn from external sources into an arbitrarily chosen dialectical scheme.[11]

Findlay holds that the triads of the dialectic vary in their content. That is, at times, the antithesis is the direct opposite of the thesis as in the case of being and nothing and at other times the antithesis is not the direct opposite of the thesis as in the case of the whole and parts. Also, the synthesis in a triad is not always the result of the unity of the thesis and antithesis. For instance, the category of becoming is shown as emerging out of the unity of being and nothing. But the development of the notion of teleology seems to have emerged out of the antithesis, namely, the chemical process alone but not out of the reconciliation between the thesis, viz., mechanical and the anti-thesis, viz., the chemical processes. So, the transitions are indefinite and a mere passing onto another term. Thus Hegel changes his dialectical device from section to section and from triad to triad and thereby riddles the method with inconsistency and render it less systematic and rigorous.[12]

Findlay maintains that the form of Hegelian dialectic is not independent of its content that it organizes, since the dialectic is largely based on the material drawn from ordinary experience, history of philosophy, nature, literature, etc. Even the Science of Logic which proposes to study concepts in the medium of pure thought is ridden with notions employed

11. Findlay, J. N., Loc. cit., p. 70.
12 Ibid., p. 74.

in the empirical science of Hegel's own days. The wheels and cranks of the dialectic operate with unction of the lubricant of experience secretly applied to it.[13]

One of the important objections of Hegelian dialectic is that the transition from Logic to Nature is unclear and absurd. Hegel holds that the Idea at the end of the sphere of Logic is complete within itself; it is itself 'something'; there is no need for an aid from external reality. Then where is the need for the extension of the dialectic into the realm of Nature ? Hegel was led to the treatment of Nature not by dialectical necessity but by the profound influence the conception of the biblical trinity exercised upon him. Thus the transition from Idea to Nature is hardly more than the formulation of a fact without a reason for it.[14] Further, it is held that though the Hegelian dialectic treats the forms of Nature as a totality and without prejudice, has failed to explain the variety of Nature in clear terms. His treatment of the forms of Nature is confusing. Hegel himself admits that confusion is the essence of Nature. But the dialectic has not done its duty of eradicating the confusion arising out of the multifarious forms of Nature.[15] And Hegel's assertion that the treatment of Nature is an apriori construction is not true, for it is based on the knowledge in the field of physics, biology, history etc. It is nothing but experience of Nature transformed into thought.[16]

It is held that Hegel's dialectic raises the super structure of his extraordinary system on the false and untrue foundation of "being" for the "being" is merely asserted but not

13. Ibid., p. 75
14. Alexander, S., *Hegel's Conception of Nature, Mind,* Vol. XL, 1886, p. 516.
15. Ibid., p. 517
16. Ibid., p. 496.

deduced out of logical necessity. The "being" is an arbitrary and contingent category which, according to Hegel, is equivalent to pure nothing. And deducing everything out of pure nothing is fantastic. If the first principle is abstract and empty, deduction of everything from it is only a make-believe.

And it is quite unintelligible to say that being and nothing are both opposed and identical to each other when they are entirely devoid of determinations. In fact, being and nothing can neither be opposed nor identical when they are underminable. And the deduction of the category of "becoming" is impossible, since the combination of being and nothing is out of question when they are undeterminable. Thus "becoming" too is not deduced necessarily but arbitrarily asserted.[17]

As mentioned already, triadicity is the fundamental principle of Hegelian dialectic. But Hegel is not consistent in observing this principle. He overlooks it whenever it is not possible for him to derive three categories from a preceding one. For example, Hegel in Logic deduces only two categories viz., "origination" and "decease" from the category of becoming.* Whereas, he deduces four types of judgments, viz., judgment of quality, quantity, relation and modality as the sub-categories of the category of judgment.** So also he deduces four kinds of syllogisms viz., qualitative syllogism,

---

17. Krishnaswamy Iyer, K. A., *Vedanta or the Scientific Reality*, Adhyatma Prakasa Karyalaya, Mysore, 1965 p. 399.

* See page 23 for the detailed discussion of the categories of "origination" and "decease".

** See page 60 for the detailed discussion of the categories of judgment.

quantitative syllogism, reflective syllogism and syllogism of necessity as the sub-categories of the category of syllogism.* Hegel commits the same mistake at several places in his 'Philosophy of Nature'. For instance, the notion of space exhibits two determinations viz., discreteness and concreteness.** But he divides the notion of physics of particular individuality into four sub-notions viz., specific gravity, cohesion, sound and warmth.*** Whereas the notion of vertebrate is divided into four sub-notions viz., fish, amphibia, birds and mammals.****

Not with standing the above objections, Hegel's dialectic is highly significant. The dialectical genius of Hegel cannot be mitigated. His achievements as a dialectician cannot be underestimated. Indeed, no other philosopher can claim to have achieved anything so considerable. His system for ever carries contemporary relevance since the dialectic is a proven method of discovering and describing the truth. The virtue of it is that it accommodates the opposite point of view and eliminates the rigid and onesided approach of understanding. It exposes the so-called independence of the philosophical concepts and brings about a correlation among them. It solves philosophical puzzles by establishing an inter-relationship between philosophical concepts. It transforms the independent concepts into notions that are interdependent. It reveals that

---

* See page 64 for the detailed discussion of the concept of syllogism.

** See page 94 for the detailed discussion of the notion of space.

*** See page 103 for the discussion of the notion of physics of particular individuality.

**** See page 116 for the discussion of the notion of vertebrate.

everything is implicity other than itself. It is the principle which unites everything with its opposite, its other by driving it beyond its immediacy. It reconciles opposed characteristics of the categories and makes them necessarily pass into each other; it reveals the truth that each category requires the other. And it shows that even a notion of freedom entails necessity. Dialectic brings to light the complementary character of the real and immanent connection between its various alternatives. Infact, the dialectical principle of the identity of opposites stresses the inter-connection as the overwhelming truth of the universe. Thus the dialectic takes us to an intrinsic nature of things.

Dialectic is the underlying principle of all movement and activity of the reality. Everything that is around us can be treated as an instance of dialectic. It shows that all that is seemingly stable and finite is an aspect of the changeable and ultimate. As already mentioned in the body of the thesis, dialectic is allpervading. It manifests in our daily life, in political revolutions and in the movements of heavenly bodies. Every event in the universe carries a contradictory of itself The dialectical contradiction is the motive force of the reality of the world. It is also the principle of movement of all philosophical thinking; it eradicates the hard and fast notions and fixed presuppositions from philosophical enterprise by bringing about an interconnection between them.

The dialectic may not possess the absolute rigour of mathematics and the experimental proof of the positive sciences. But one has to judge the dialectic for what it is but not for what one thinks it ought to be. The significance of the dialectical method consists in illuminating the forms of factual knowledge by philosophical notions. It shows an ingeneous blend of factual knowledge and philosophical notions. Its aim is not to disrupt the seeming order of the philosophical concepts but to attain everricher states of equilibrium by eradicating the immediacy of sense perception and unreflective reasonableness of understanding. Dialectic deepens our conceptual grasp by revealing the fact that notions possess a 'logical dynamic' which determines and propels them to move forward.

Indeed, Hegel's work, in its method, in its purpose and in its execution is unique in the history of philosophy. Such an exhaustive and elaborate treatment of thought, nature and history wrs certainly not attempted before. Hegel alone can be credited with the herculian and successful task of embodying the knowledge of epic scope in a single system which amply testifies to Hegel's serious commitment to genuine philosophy.

The study of Hegel's writings is often interpreted as amounting to an intellectual crucifixion. But an ardent lover of philosophy always finds such a crucifixion highly worthwhile and rewarding. A critic who is not overlaid by prejudice and misconception is bound to admit that the omniscience and novelty of Hegel's work has contributed immensely to the development of philosophy.

BIBLIOGRAPHY

Adorno, Theodor, W.	: Negative Dialectics, Routledge & Kegan Paul Ltd., London, 1973.
Althusser, Louis	: For Marx, Verso, London, 1979.
Anderson, Perry	: Considerations on Western Marxism, Verso, London, 1979.
Auineri, Schlomo	: Hegel's Theory of the Modern State, Cambridge University Press, Cambridge, 1972.
Bencivenga, Eramno	: Kant's Copernican Revolution, Oxford University Press, 1987.
Bently, John Edward	: Visual outilne of Philosophy, Longman Gren & Co., New York.
Bernard, Reardon, M.G.	: Hegel's Philosophy of Religion, Macmillan Co., Ltd., London, 1977.
Blackham, H. J.	: Six-Existentialist Thinkers, Routledge & Kegan Paul Ltd., London, 1961.
Burnet, John	: Early Greek Philosophy, Adam & Charles Black, London, 4th edition 1930 & Reprint 1952.
Caird, Edward	: Hegel London & Edinburgh, 1883.

Coletti, Lucio : Marxism and Hegel, Translated by Lawrence Garner, Verso, London, 1973.

Cornford, Francis Macdonald : Plato's Theory of Knowledge, The Theaetetus and the Sophist of Plato, Routledge & Kegan Paul Ltd., London, 1957.

Cornforth, Maurice : Dialectical Materialism : An Introduction Course, 3 Vols., Lawrence & Wishart Ltd., London, 1952.

Croce, Benedetto : What is Living and What is Dead in the Philosophy of Hegel Translated by Douglas Ainslic, London, 1915.

Crosman, R.H.S. : Government and the Governed, Chatto and Windus, London, 1969.

Deleuze, Gilles : Kant's Critical Philosophy; The Doctrine of Faculties, Athlone press, London, 1984.

Della Volpe, Galvano : Rousseau and Marx, Lawrence & Wishart, London, 1978.

Dickey, Laurence : Hegel Religion, Economics and the Politics of Spirit, 1770-1807, Cambridge University Press, Cambridge, 1987.

Engels, F. : Dialectics of Nature, Progress Publishers, Moscow, 1974.

——— Ludwig Feuerbach and the end of Classical German Philosophy, Progress Publishers, Moscow.

Erdmann, Johann, E. : A History of Philosophy, Vol. III, Translated by W.S. Hough, London & New York, 1890.

Falckenberg, Richard : History of Modern Philosophy, Progressive Publishers, Calcutta, 1977.

Fichte, J. G. : Science of Knowledge, Translated and edited by P. Heath J. Lachs, Cambridge University Press, 1982.

——— : Science of Rights, Tr. A. E. Kroegar, Routledge and Kegan Paul Ltd., London, 1970.

Findlay, J. N. : Hegel : A Re-Examination, George Allen & Unwin Ltd., London, 1958.

Frederick, S.J. Copleston : A History of Philosophy, Vol. 7, Modern Philosophy, Part I, Fichte & Hegel, Image Books, New York, 1954.

Friendrich, Carl. J. : The Philosophy of Hegel, The Modern Library, New York, 1954.

Gadamer : Hegel's Dialectic, Five Hermeneutical Studies, Tr. by Christopher Smith, Yale University Press, London, 1971.

Godelier, Maurice : Rationality and Irrationality in Economics, Monthly Review Press, New York, 1972.

Gomperz, Theodor : Greek Thinkers, A History of Ancient Philosophy, 4 Vols.

John Murry, Albemarle Street, W. London, First Edition—1901 Reprint 1955.

Gray, C. J., Glenn : Hegel's Hellenic Ideal, Kings Crown Press, New York, 1941.

Hamilton Edith and Huntington Cairns (ed.) : The Collected Dialogues of Plato Including the Letters Princeton University Press, New Jersey, USA.

——— : The Collected Dialogues of Plato Bollingen series XXI, Princeton University Press, New Jersey, 1973.

Harris, H.S. : Hegel's Development, Toward the Sunlight 1770-1801, Clarendon Press, Oxford, 1972.

Harris, W.T. : Hegel's Logic Chicago, 1895.

Haulgate, Stephen : Hegel Nietzsche and the Criticism of Metaphysics, Cambridge University Press, Cambridge, 1986.

Hegel, G.W.F. : Aesthetics-Lectures on Fine Art, 2 Vols. Translated by T. M. Knox, Clarendon Press, London, 1975.

——— : The Difference between the Fichtean and Schellingean Systems of Philosophy. Tr. Surber, Jene Paul, Ridgeview Publishing Company, California, 1978.

———— : Encyclopaedia of Philosophy, Translated and annotated by G.E. Mueller, New York, 1929.

———— : Lectures on the History of Philosophy, 3 Vols., Translated by E. S. Haldane & F. H. Simpson, Routledge & Kegan Paul Ltd., London, 1955.

———— : Lectures on the Philosophy of Religion together with a work on the Proofs of the Existence of God, 3 Vols., Translated by E.B. Speris and J. B. Sanderson, London, 1895, Reprint 1962.

———— : Lectures on the Philosophy of World History, Translated by H.B. Nibset, Cambridge University Press, Cambridge, London, 1975.

———— : Science of Logic, 2 Vols., Translated by W. H. Johnston and L. G. Struthers, George Allen & Unwin Ltd., London, IInd impression, 1951.

———— : The Science of Logic, Translated by A.V. Miller, George Allen & Unwin Ltd., London, 1969.

———— : Phenomenology of Mind, Translated by J. B. Baillie, George Allen & Unwin Ltd., London, 2nd edition, 1949.

———— : Philosophy of Nature, 3 Vols., Translated and edited by Petry, M.J., George Allen & Unwin Ltd., London, 1970.

———— : Philosophy of Mind Translated by William Wallace, Clarenden Press, London, 1894.

———— : Philosophy of Right, Translated by T.M.Knox, Clarendon Press, London, 1967.

Hook, Sidney : From Hegel to Marx : Studies the Intellectual Development of Karl Marx, The Humanities Press, New York, 1950.

Hunt, R.W. Carew : The Theory and Practice of in Communism, Penguin, 1977.

Ilyenkor, E.V. : Dialectical Logic Progress Publishers, Moscow, 1977.

Iyer, K.A. Krishnaswamy : Vedanta or the Science of Reality, Adhyatma Prakasha Karyalaya, Holenarsipur, Mysose, India, Revised edition 1965.

Jackson, T.A. : Dialectics—The Logic of Marxism and its Criticism an Essay in Exploration, Oriental Publishing House, Benaras, First Indian Reprint 1945.

Jonathan, Bennet : Kant's Analytic, Cambridge University Press, 1966.

——— : Kant's Dialectic, Cambridge University Press, Cambridge, 1974.

Kant, Immanuel : Critique of Pure Reason, Translated by Norman Kemp Smith. Macmillan & Co. Ltd., London, 1963.

Kharin, Yu, A. : Fundamentals of Dialectics, Progress Publishers, Moscow, 1981.

Kneale, William and Martha Kneale : The Development of Logic, The Clarendon Press, Oxford, 1962.

Kojene, Alexander : Introduction to the Reading of Hegel, Translated by J. H. Nichols, New York, 1969.

Lamb, David : Hegel—From Foundation to System, Martinus Wifhooff Publishers, London, 1980.

Lenin, V. I. : Collected Works, Vol. 1 and 38, Foreign Language Publishing House, Moscow, 1963.

——— : Materialism and Empirio, Criticism, Progress Publishers, Moscow, 1977.

——— : On Trade Unions, Progress Publishers, Moscow, 1978.

——— : On the Question of Dialectics : A Collection, Progress Publishers, Moscow, 1982.

Lenine, Norman : Dialogue within the Dialectic, George Allen & Unwin Ltd., London, 1984.

Lowenberg, Jocob (ed) : Hegel—Selections, Charles Sribners & Sons, New York, 1957.

Lowith, Karl : From Hegel to Nietzsche, Tr. by David E. Green, New York, 1964.

Lukacs, Georg : History and Class Consciousness, Merlin Press, London, 1971.

——— : The Young Hegel, Merlin Press, London, 1975.

Mckeon, Richard (ed) : Introduction to Aristotle, University of Chicago Press, Chicago and London, 1973.

Mackintosh, R. : Hegel and Hegelianism, T & T Clark, Edinburgh, 1903.

MacIyntre, Alasdair (ed) : Hegel; A Collection of Critical Essays, Gardencity, New York, Double day, 1972.

Marcuse, Herbert : Reason and Revolution, Routledge and Kegan Paul Ltd., London, 1954.

McTaggart, J.M.E. : Commentary on Hegel's Logie Cambridge University Press, Cambridge, IInd edition, 1922.

Marx, Karl : Capital, 3 Vols., Progress Publishers, Moscow, 1977.

——— ; The Holy Family, Progress Publishers, Moscow.

Marx, Karl : Capital, 3 Vols., Progress Publishers, Moscow, 1977

Marx, Engles and Lenin : On dialectical Materialism, Progress Publishers, Moscow, 1977

Mehta, V. R. : Hegel and the Modern State : An Introduction to Hegel's Political Thought. Associated Publishing House, New Delhi, 1968.

Mure, G.R.G. : An Introduction to Hegel, Clarendon Press, Oxford, London, Reprint, 1948.

———— : A Study of Hegel's Logic, Oxford, 1950.

Norman, Richard and Seen Sayers : Hegel, Marx and Dialectic : A Debate, Humanity Press, New Jersey, 1980.

O' Brien, George Dennise : Hegel on Reason and History, The University of Chicago Press, Chicago, 1975.

Oizerman, Theodore : Dialectical Materialism and the History of Philosophy, Progress Publishers, Moscow, 1982.

Orynski, Wanda : Hegel Highlights : An Annotated Selection, Wisdom Library, A Division of Philosophical Library, New York, 1960.

Pattison, Pringle and A. Seth : Hegelianism and Personality, London, 1893, 2nd edition.

Pelozynski (ed) : The State and Civil Society, Studies in Hegel's Political

Philosophy, Cambridge University Press, Cambridge, 1987.

Plato : Republic, Translated by Francis Macdonald Cornford, Clarendon Press, Oxford, 1955.

Plamenatz, John, : Man and Society, 2 Vols., London, 1963.

Plekhanov, G.V. : Selected Philosophical Works, Vol. I, Progress Publishers, Moscow, 1974.

Popper, Karl, R. : Conjectures and Refutations, Routledge & Kegan Paul Ltd., London, 1981.

——— : The Open Society and its Enemies, 2 Vols., Routledge & Kegan Paul Ltd., London, IInd edition, 1952.

Prasad, Rama : Ramanuja and Hegel, A Comparative Study, Classical Publishing Company, New Delhi, 1983.

Priest, Stephen : Hegel's Critique of Kant, Clarendon Press, Oxford, 1987.

Progress Publishers (ed) : Philosophy in the USSR : Problems of Dialectical Materialism, Progress Publishers, Moscow, 1977.

Raymond, Plant : Hegel, George Allen & Unwin Ltd., London, 1973.

Richard, Robinson : Plato's Earlier Dialectics, Clarendon Press, Oxford, 1953.

Riedel, Manfred : Between Tradition and Revolution, The Hegelian Transformation of Political Philosophy, Cambridge University Press, Cambridge, New York, 1984.

Rosen, Stanley : G.W.F. Hegel : Introduction to the Science of Wisdom, Yale Univeasity Press, London, 1974.

Ross, W.D. (ed) : The Works of Aristotle 12 Vols. Clarendon Press, Oxford, Reprint, 1953.

Russell, Bertrand : History of Western Philosophy and its Connection with Political and Social Circumstances from the Earliest Times to the Present Day. George Allen & Unwin Ltd., London, 1975.

——— : The Problems of Philosophy, Oxford University Press, London, Oxford, New York, Reprint, 1974.

Sartre, Jean Paul : Critique of Dialectical Reason. New Left Books, London, 1976.

Schroeder, Willian Ralph : Sartre and his Predecessors Routledge & Kegan Paul Ltd., London, 1984.

Seth, Andrew : Hegelianism and Personality, Universities, Edinburgh, Balfar, Philosophical lectures.

Stace, W.T. : A Critical History of Greek Philosophy, Macmilian India Ltd., Delhi, Bombay, Calcutta, Madras, 1982.

——— : The Philosophy of Hegel, Dover Publications, New York, 1955.

Stalin, Joseph : Dialectical and Historical Materialism, New Book Centre, Calcutta, 1976.

Starlemijn, Andries : Hegel's Dialectic, D. Reidel Publishing Company, Boston USA, 1971.

Steinkraus, Warren (ed) : New Studies in Hegel's Philosophy, Holt, Rinehart and Neinston, Inc., New York, 1971.

Sterrett J. Machridge : Studies in Hegel's Philosophy of Religion, Swan Sonnenschein & Co., London, 1891.

Strawson, P. F. : The Bounds of Sense, Methuen & Co., London, 1973.

Stumpf, Samuel Enoch : Socrates to Sartre, McGraw Hill Press, America, 1975.

Taylor, A. E. : Aristotle, Dover Publications, New York, Inc. 1955.

Taylor, Charles : Hegel, Cambridge University Press, London, 1978.

——— : Hegel and Modern Society, Cambridge University Press, Cambridge, 1979.

Toews, John Edward : Hegelianism the Path toward Dialectical Humanism 1805-1841 Cambridge University Press, Cambridge, 1980.

Travis, D.C. (ed) : A Hegel Symposium, Austin Texas, 1962.

Tucker, C. Robert ; Philosophy and Myth in Karl Marx, Cambridge University Press, Cambridge, 1961.

Wallace, W. : Prolegomena to the Study of Hegel's Philosophy and especially of his Logic, Oxford, 1894.

———— : Logic of Hegel, Oxford University Press, London, IInd edition, 1968.

Walsh, W. H. : The Origines of Hegelianism in Metaphysics, London, 1963.

Walter, Kaufmann : From Shakespeare to Existentialism, Princeton University Press, New Jersey, 1980.

———— : Hegel : Reinterpretation, Texts and Commentaries, Weidenfeld Nicolson, London, 1966.

———— : The Young Hegel and Religion, Boston, 1959.

Wedberg, Anders : A History of Philosophy, 2 Vols., Clarendon Press, Oxford, 1970.

Werner, Marx : Hegel's Phenomenology of Spirit Its point and phrase—A Commentary on the Preface and Introduction, Harper & Row, New York.

Windleband, W. : History of Ancient Philosophy, Translated by Herbert Ernest Cushman, Dover Publications, Inc. USA, 1956.

Yovel, Yirmiahu : Kant and the Philosophy of History, Princeton University Press, 1980.

Zeller, Eduard : Outlines of the History of Greet Philosophy, Translated by L.R. Palmer, Routledge & Kegan Paul Ltd., London, VIII edition, 1931, Reprint, 1950.

JOURNALS

Cambridge Review, Cambridge University Press, Cambridge, Vol. 94, 1972.

Journal of the History of Ideas, Ephrata pa Inc., 1979.

Journal of the History of Philosophy (Berkelay), California, Vol. 16 (1978).

Marxism Today, Communist Party of Great Britain, London, Vol. 21, 1977.

Mind, Williams and Norgate, London, Vols. I-1892. III-1894, VI-1897, VII-1898, VIII-1899, IX-1900, X-1901, XI-1902. XII-1903, XIII-1904, XVII-1908, XVIII-1914, XLIV-1935, XLIX-1940, New Series, Vol. 43 (1934.)

The Monist, The Edward Hegeler foundation La Salle, Illinois, 48 (1964).

Personalist, The School of Philosophy, The University of Southern California, Los Angels, California, Vol. XLIX, 1968.

Philosophy, The Journal of Royal Institute of Philosophy, Macmillan & Co. Ltd., London.

Philosophy and Phenomenalogical Research, The University of Buffalo Foundation, New York, Vols. XLVII, 1986, XLVIII, June, 1987.

Philosophical Review, Cornell University, Ithaca, New York, Vols. XLVI, 1937, XLVIII-1939.